Mindful Money
Matters

Mindful Money
Matters

8 Ways to Honor Yourself
and Your Financial Plan

Susan Zimmerman, ChFC, LMFT

Mindful Money Matters:

8 Ways to Honor Yourself and Your Financial Plan

This publication is designed to provide accurate and authoritative information regarding the subject matter covered. If expert assistance or counseling is needed, the services of a competent professional should be sought. Except for the author's own stories, none of the people depicted in the case vignettes are real persons, nor are they meant to resemble anyone living or deceased.

ISBN: 978-1-946195-14-2
Library of Congress Number: 2017947551

Printed in the United States of America

22 21 20 19 18   5 4 3 2 1

Publisher: Mindful Asset Publishing

Editor: Bill Perron
Illustrator: Caroline Wolf
Cover Design: Jean Kindem
Interior Design: Integrative Ink
Photographer: Rod Wilson

Advanced Praise

"It's not often you get a chance to learn from a pioneer and Susan is certainly a pioneer when it comes to blending psychology with financial planning. Susan's insightful and witty exploration of the possible motives behind money behavior, and the communication tips she provides, are valuable tools for making sound money decisions."

Rick Kahler, MSFP, CFP®
President, Kahler Financial Group
Co-author of *Conscious Finance, The Financial Wisdom of Ebenezer Scrooge* and *Wired For Wealth*

"Susan shares a powerful 'wealth-being' philosophy and set of practices that will help you think differently and honor what matters most to you when it comes to managing money issues and growing wealth. Mindful Money practices will help you attract peace and prosperity to your life."

Mark LeBlanc
Small Business Success
Author of *Growing Your Business* and *Never Be the Same*

"Many smart people are aware of a strong connection between emotions and money, but Susan demonstrates a new level of genius when it comes to understanding and addressing the mind-money connection to improve overall well-being. The timing of this book could not be better! Behavioral finance researchers clearly show

that individuals are subject to cognitive and emotional biases that may lead to suboptimal financial decisions, but few have written on how to overcome maladaptive thoughts and behaviors. Susan should be commended for innovatively addressing this challenging (but incredibly important) topic!"

Joseph Goetz, Ph.D.
2013 President, Financial Therapy Association
Associate Professor of Financial Planning,
University of Georgia

"I love what Susan has put together! She artfully expands the topic of money beyond the numbers to the hidden belief systems behind it. Susan not only creates understanding, but provides tools for the sensitive, yet ever present, topic of money."

Cheryl Leitschuh, Ed.D., RCC
Leadership Energy Consultant, Author of the top-selling book,
Leadership Energy: Unlocking the Secrets to Your Success

"Susan gives us practical applications and efficient techniques to identify emotional drivers and provide action steps to make the most of our human and financial assets. Thank you for this great resource, Susan. Bravo!"

Janet A. Stanzak, CFP®, MS, Principal
Financial Empowerment LLC
FPA President 2014

"Susan's work provides solid stepping stones to help us step more comfortably and effectively into the arena of emotions and money. Her acronyms and money motives are excellent tools to help segue into therapeutic communication and positive change. Intriguing and easy to follow, these methods have real merit!"

Dave Jetson, MS
Jetson Counseling
Author of *Finding Emotional Freedom: Access the Truth Your Brain Already Knows*

"Susan's book is an excellent training guide for integrating Mindful Money practices into your financial planning strategies. Her whole process integrates smoothly into self-awareness and decision-making that aligns with true motives and values."

Martin Kurtz, CFP®, Founder/President
The Planning Center
FPA President 2011

"The practical application possibilities abound in Susan's memorable and easy to read guide. Her distinctive acronyms with descriptive examples make it easy to envision and use. Anyone in the pursuit of financial well-being can apply these beneficial techniques and resources."

Sarah D. Asebedo, Ph.D., CFP®
Assistant Professor
Texas Tech University

TABLE OF CONTENTS

Acknowledgments xi

1 | Mindful Money Matters 1

2 | Your Money Personality................................15

3 | Reconstruction Zone................................29

4 | 8 Therapeutic Acronyms 41

    AHA: Action Honoring Awareness 43

    ACE: Ask – Confirm – Encourage 49

    GEM: Generate Empowered Movement 51

    HIRE: Halt – Inhale – Reflect – Elect 53

    COOL/FOOL Rules 55

    TINT: This Is Not That 57

    TWEDY: To What Extent Do You 59

    NEAR: Numb–Emotional–Adjusting–Rebuilding 61

5 | Money Motive #1 — Prestige 63

6 | Money Motive #2 — Spontaneity 73

7 | Money Motive #3 — Peace 83

8 | Money Motive #4 — Simplicity 91

9 | Money Motive #5 — Virtue 101

10 | Money Motive #6 — Security 111

11 | Money Motive #7 — Control 119

12 | Money Motive #8 — Growth 127

13 | Conflict Resolution 135

14 | ABC's of Raising "Fiscally Fit" Kids 155

15 | Brain Science & Mindful Prosperity 161

16 | Take Heart in Mindful Money Matters 177

References 183

ACKNOWLEDGMENTS

First and foremost, I want to thank our clients for their inspiration and determination in working with us over the past 30 years. They've been the #1 source of encouragement and feedback as we braved to integrate mindfulness methodologies into our financial planning practices. It took courage on both our parts, as we were ahead of our time in blending money and psychology together. Our clients have always been the first people who were willing and eager to participate in our therapeutic acronyms, genogram process, and other exercises for increased self-awareness and attentiveness. Their gratitude and expression of insights in our mindful money conversations have been invaluable.

The process of creating the tools featured in this book is the result of ongoing formal education and discussions with professional leaders in psychology and financial planning. I want to thank the Adler Graduate School of Psychology for their tremendous curriculum and continuing education. A special thank you is also extended to our talented Mindful Asset Planning team for their ongoing support and contribution to our mindful money tools. We continue to be deeply grateful for the educational programs in our professional associations, which include the National Association of Professional Financial Advisors, the Financial Planning Association, the Financial Therapy Association, the Nazrudin Project, the Association of Financial Counseling and Planning Education, the National Speakers Association, the American Psychological Association, and the American Association of Marriage and Family Therapists.

I want to especially thank my professional colleagues for their ongoing research and work in support of financial psychology. As I discovered in meeting them at various conferences after I'd developed materials to blend the two subjects, they, too, had been researching and speaking about it. Thank you to Rick Kahler, for his brilliance and dedication to blending financial planning and psychology. For his founding leadership in the Nazrudin Project and the Financial Therapy Association, I want to thank Dick Wagner. Sadly, Dick passed away this past year. Rick Kahler stated it well, "The financial planning profession to which Dick devoted so much of his life was vastly enriched by his ideas and his work." Thank you also to Joe Goetz and Kristy Archuleta for their dedication in expanding the profession of financial therapy.

We are continuously grateful to our family members for their support of our work. My marriage and business partner of 30 years, Steve, has been an enthusiast for this work through every stage of its development. Our adult children inspire us with their financial wellness and are never shy about providing feedback on what financial planning lessons are most valuable to them. In other words, our children and their young children keep us on our toes now as much as ever before!

This book wouldn't have been possible without the incredible team of professionals who contributed their talent to its production. Thank you to Bill Perron for his smart editing. Special thanks to Jean Kindem for her book cover design and to photographer Rod Wilson. And to Caroline Wolf, thank you for enthusiastically illustrating each money rascal with your wonderful, creative flair.

1

Mindful Money Matters

Several years ago, when I began writing and speaking about "Mindful Money" at educational conferences, mindfulness hadn't been associated with money. Mindful Money, when paired together, I would explain, is the concept of combining deepened psychological awareness and behavioral attentiveness with financial planning matters.

Each of us has a unique pattern, or set of motivations, that drive our financial choices. When we more fully understand our own histories and the interpretations we've given them, it creates a heightened consciousness that integrates well into the ongoing decisions we make in our lifelong personal financial planning.

Mindful Money Matters has dual meaning:

1. *Being mindful* about money, most definitely, matters a great deal! It matters, in that it makes a significant difference in outcomes when we operate in full, alert awareness of our financial direction and decision-making process.

2. Mindful *money matters* and issues are integrated into sound financial planning. These include basic financial principles such as managing cash flow, spending, saving, the time value of money, the use of tax savings strategies, investment allocations, and regular reviews of progress made with changes that are necessary to stay on target. Mindful money matters include integrating the importance of our human assets into our financial strategies. Human assets include our historic and future financial styles and preferences, interests, values, career identities, goals, and important relationships, to name a few.

When we learn to observe ourselves from flexible perspectives, it frees us to adjust our thinking and behavior with greater ease. Many topics related to financial decisions—emotions, thoughts, and habits—arise when discussing money matters. These include but are not limited to:

- Family communication dynamics
- Individual habits and outlooks
- Bill paying and the use of credit

- Spending decisions
- Defining the concept of "enough"
- Special needs for parents, children, or others
- Career decisions
- Societal expectations vs. personal preferences
- Cash flow organization and budgeting
- Risk management
- Power dynamics
- Couples' communication
- Conflict resolution
- Mental and physical health issues
- Employee benefits and insurance
- Retirement savings and investments
- Retirement timing decisions
- Investment risk tolerance
- Managing worries, disappointment, and expectations
- Decisions about contributing to children's education
- Dealing with an adult child's financial problems
- Estate planning questions and preferences
- Social pressures and image issues
- Vacations, recreation, and entertainment
- Generalized anxiety and worries
- Control and structure
- Financial analysis and assumptions
- Inflation and other factors
- Almost infinite other money matters!

Honoring Yourself *and* Your Financial Plan

To honor something means to pay it great respect. Honor also means honesty or integrity in one's beliefs and actions. It's vital to know that you can respect your own historic style and preference with money, while also simultaneously honoring your financial plan. The two aren't mutually exclusive. When you **honor a balance** between the two, both function more harmoniously and become easier to do. Keep in mind, balance rarely means equal, and no two people are identical in their version of the best balance for them. The key is in finding what uses of money matter most to you, so you can prioritize them for your current life. That way, you're less likely to unintentionally neglect planning for your future financial needs.

The purpose of the *Mindful Money Matters* book is to serve as a map that guides you into becoming increasingly aware and attentive in your financial life. It will help you make meaningful connections in your own personal financial history, perhaps even reflecting on some childhood memories that influenced your pattern of thoughts and behaviors around money.

When you are conscious of your values and use them to guide your financial choices, it's easier to build a grounded and consciously aware perspective at each stage of your life. You'll find the mindful discovery process tools in this book help you understand your past decisions and inform those in your future.

Adventure in Financial Psychology

The best way to think of financial psychology is to view it as an adventure in self-awareness relative to your financial thoughts, emotions, and actions. By positioning the process as an adventure, it creates greater openness and receptivity to discovering the impact of your life experiences in your money life. It helps you identify and navigate changes you decide to make.

In the mid-nineties, my eighth year as a financial planner, many of the people I was counseling had been referred by marriage therapists. The financial conflicts with which they struggled had often escalated over time. The emotions that accompanied the frustration and stress from unresolved problems had also intensified.

Financial planning education and credentials were essential for solving financial puzzles, but seemed quite limited when it came to solving human emotional puzzles. Conflict resolution skills weren't part of the financial planning curricula, so I began graduate school in psychology to bridge that gap. My research of societal and family systems' influences on financial behavior became an important bridge into creating tools that could help. Increased self-awareness often spurred growth in financial resources and life satisfaction.

I adapted the psychological theories and practices taught to issues I'd seen arise in the context of financial planning discussions. Financial psychology was essentially unheard of during those mid-nineties years, but when I brought it up with people, their interest was immediate and significant. That fueled my continued research.

Financial conflict can arise in relationships but also within oneself. It's not unusual to have two opposing preferences within your own money personality that conflict with each other. This internal conflict is characterized by the money rascal known as Clasher, named for clashing unresolved internal conflicts over various financial matters. The study of financial psychology, especially when paired with financial analysis, can help resolve dilemmas.

Mindful Money for Wealth and Well-Being

Mindful Money for Wealth and Well-Being was the earlier version of this book, written for financial and social service professionals in 2014. Investment News magazine named it as #1 "must read" that year. *Mindful Money Matters* is an updated version of that book, tailored for individual use as you engage in your personal financial planning. This book covers the same topics as the practitioner's version, but focuses on how you can use the same therapeutic tools to explore your money personality dynamics as they impact your own personal financial life planning.

Striking a balance of wealth and well-being is at its core an ongoing therapeutic process. The subject of wealth can seem like an unappealing topic, as it sometimes represents many inequities and injustices in our society. It takes effortful wisdom to keep going and not give up when faced with what sometimes seems to be insurmountable complexity or other obstacles.

At our firm, Mindful Asset Planning (MAP), we created a definition of wealth that includes the psychological importance of well-being:

> *"Wealth means to make the absolute most of your human and financial assets."*

Consciously adding your human assets to your operational awareness often provides a boost in overall life assets. Human assets include your health, loved ones, talents, interests, values, positive attitude, energy, and effort. Your human assets should guide what you do with your financial assets. When the two are in alignment, you'll be better able to overcome obstacles, achieve goals, and enjoy life. It helps you bring the best of yourself to others. This, in turn, multiplies societal well-being as people positively affect each other.

An additional note about MAP: We used the word "Asset" for two reasons:

1. *Asset* has a holistic definition; it means resource or advantage. We'd been sharing the advantages of integrating both human assets and financial assets into life planning discussions for many years. Our clients see this combination as an overall advantage

in the insights they've gained by having this balance to help guide their decisions.

2. ***Asset*** allowed for the creation of a meaningful company name – ***MAP*** – that aligns with our firms' message, "Helping you *MAP* a more prosperous path." We all benefit with a good map to help direct us to our determined destination. That's a vital first step – determining where we're trying to go. From there, without a map, it's easy to get lost and take costly wrong turns when we're guessing at what roads will get us to our destination. The Mad Hatter from *Alice in Wonderland* reflected great wisdom when he said, "Any road will get you there if you don't know where you're going!" A *mindful money* process helps MAP a strategy that clarifies the destinations, identifies the best paths for getting there, and makes the journey more enjoyable along the way.

Mindfulness and Beyond

After we'd begun using the phrase *mindful money* and built it into our company identity, I began discovering Mindfulness in other arenas. It has many "homes." It had become a frequent subject in continuing education courses for psychology and mental health practitioners. It's been incorporated into psychological theories and therapies. It's also embedded in modern neuroscience. And of course, it resides in its original form in the spiritual lessons of Buddhism.

A full examination of all areas of mindfulness is beyond the scope of this book. However, in a later chapter titled, "Brain Science & Mindful Prosperity," I've integrated some of the basic elements of brain science and practical applications of it. In the resources section, you'll see several books and experts in this area that I highly recommend if you want a more in depth understanding of scientific or spiritual mindfulness.

First Came Mindless

Nobody starts life being consciously mindful of anything. If we're lucky, our survival needs are provided for and our biological instincts cooperate to help us survive and thrive. In this sense, we are "mindless" before we're "mindful." A simple and nonclinical definition of mindful means aware. Pragmatically speaking, in the context of financial planning, it also means attentive. When we purposefully heighten our awareness of something, it's important to attend to it in new and improved ways.

As we mature and begin to use money, we develop impressions of what it is about. In childhood, we witness transactions before we have any clear awareness of money's origin or relativity. Initially, our knowledge about money is essentially that it's used in exchange for receiving goods and services.

Growing into adulthood, we gather multiple experiences with money, but we often remain predominantly mindless (unaware) about how to manage it well. A psychology class quoted the phrase, "Mindless is blindness." This is a useful contextual reminder that we can't see what's hidden from view.

> In a very real way, the goal of *mindful money* is to transform money mystery into money mastery – for peace of mind and improved financial well-being.

Most people have a few blind spots with money. Knowing what matters *is* what matters! As financial practitioners, we help our clients determine what matters most to them at various stages of their lives, and how to use their total resources to create the best results possible. It takes effort to see what's been hidden from view. In a very real way, the goal of *mindful money* is to transform money mystery into money mastery – for peace of mind and improved financial well-being.

Visualize an iceberg to conceptualize your conscious and unconscious belief systems. An awesome structure of ice broken off from a glacier and floating in the sea, much of its mass (about 90%) is beneath the surface of the water.

Unconscious thought is like the mass of ice under the water. Most of the time we don't see the submerged portion and are unaware of its influence on the iceberg. But its influence is powerful enough to move the entire mass of the iceberg.

Conscious thought is like the part of the iceberg we can see *above* the surface. We're aware of it because it's in plain view. Provided we are paying attention, we can maneuver around it to avoid damage from its jagged edges.

Because the portion of ice *below* the water is vast and hidden from view, it requires some special equipment and exploration to see it. If we remain unaware of it when it matters the most, we may unknowingly steer ourselves in a direction that causes damage (remember the Titanic)! In making our way through life, becoming aware of what lies beneath the surface of our conscious thought can help us move in a more positive direction. A "Mindful Money Map" can protect us from the jagged edges of poor choices that can sabotage our genuine needs and goals.

At any given age or life stage, we may also be unaware of the many unconscious expectations we've developed about money. These expectations range from relationship issues to spending and savings matters. It takes examination of this maze-like system of thoughts to discover our own belief systems' inaccuracies or biases.

Examples of unconscious money expectation *categories* and sample questions worth exploring is below. With each question, explore any inaccuracies you may notice in your own responses. What adjustments might you make to increase the accuracy of your expectations in your life today?

- Gender roles – Do I expect certain behaviors based on gender?
- Careers – Have my choices been about money or the work itself?
- Earnings – Do I have self-limiting beliefs about this?
- Spending priorities – How do I resolve what to say yes (or no) to?
- Savings and investments – Are the models I've followed on this still relevant?
- Decision power in relationships – Has this openly been addressed?
- Organization – How do I keep track of everything?
- Bill paying – Is there a right and a wrong way?
- Budgeting and cash flow – What organization works best for me?
- Managing debt and use of credit – Do I expect to be "in the black" or "in the red?"
- Planning for old age needs – Have I financially honored the older person I will become?
- Legacy planning – How should I think about matters beyond my own life?
- Money and self-image – What defines authentic success or failure *to me?*

- Impulsivity and control – Do I think one is better than the other?

These are just a few of the areas for which people form preferences or impressions of how things may take shape in their lives. Ponder the importance of bringing them into more conscious awareness for your planning needs.

Then Came Mindful

Keep in mind our simple definition of mindful as *"aware and attentive."* Daniel Siegel, M.D., describes it in his book, *Mindsight: The New Science of Personal Transformation.*

"Mindsight is a kind of focused attention that allows us to see the internal workings of our own minds. It helps us to be aware of our inner processes without being swept away by them, enables us to get ourselves off the autopilot of ingrained behaviors and habitual responses, and moves us beyond the reactive emotional loops we all have a tendency to get trapped in."

Staying mindful as you navigate in your financial journey can keep you from being overwhelmed if you're ever faced with multiple complexities. These can range from relationship disharmony to troubling debt. Even when things are going well, a comprehensive plan covers a lot of ground. That's why your goals are so important, as they help you overcome obstacles along the way.

It's useful to keep in mind the difference between a wish and a goal as you reflect on your own journey. Wishing for something typically doesn't carry that fire-in-the-belly commitment that makes change possible. But defining your goals and identifying specifically what it takes to achieve them, significantly increases your motivation and achievement.

The blending of mental and financial health services is growing due to recognition of the deeper and longer lasting benefits it provides.

As the cover graphics of this book convey, finding your unique money life balance can be greatly assisted with the right directional signs. The lightning bolt is a reminder to strike a balance to honor yourself without neglecting your financial planning. When you learn to live more mindfully, your customized balance becomes easier, during the ups and downs of life. When you can see with the new lens of heightened awareness, attending to money matters improves in lasting ways.

2

Your Money Personality

This book is designed to serve as a reference relative to your own dominant styles and preferences with money – your money personality. If your money could talk, what might it say to you? This is what I call the "Dollar Holler" exercise. It's a first thought on the topic of money personality.

I'll summarize the eight money motives that drive financial decisions and link them with their corresponding money rascals. The money rascals are named for the type of mischief they sometimes make that can cause problems if they become overly dominant in your decisions.

Your money personality is a highly important component of your financial well-being. The more deeply you understand your money personality's belief systems and emotions that guide your choices, the better able you are to honor your strengths and make modifications you desire.

The 8 Money Rascals and Money Motives

Eight money personalities are characterized by the most commonly recurring patterns for people. The money motives describe what internal desires drive your financial actions. The money rascals are the mischievous traits that can sometimes cause problems in your financial life. *Mindful Money Matter's* goal is to elevate your understanding both. It will help you honor and grow the strengths of each, and to change any troublesome habits from the inside out.

The eight money personality patterns include the four components of personality applied to money matters. It's helpful to think of them as 'PET' habits that have evolved into your favorites over time. The most important thing to remember is that you get to determine for yourself if your dominant money personalities need any modification to achieve improved satisfaction in your financial life.

The PETS Personality Components:

Physical – This represents your typical money handling habits. It includes your common practices around the cash you carry, but also affects credit card use, bill-paying, and the many organizational issues of personal finance.

Emotional – Here you're identifying your most common feelings about your money life. There are 3000 words in the English language that represent emotions. When it comes to money, you may have just a few that dominate. Do you tend to be calm or stressed when it comes to money? Are you confident or insecure? Or perhaps you're typically balanced and consistent. It's important to be aware of emotions, and to manage them in your personal finance, especially because they may at times mislead you into unhelpful decisions.

Thoughts – When you think about your finances, in what direction do your thoughts move? Would you say they're on the positive end of the spectrum, or do they lean toward the negative? Do you tell yourself you're capable and skilled with money, or is there some other message clanging loudly in your head?

Your belief systems are worth assessing, as they, too, may need some fresh remodeling to better fit you today.

Social – Does your financial behavior tend to shift frequently, depending on who you're with? Has that caused you to make decisions that are unhelpful to your financial health? As with the other components of personality, the social one can be modified to bring greater satisfaction and consistency for you. The best way to be in alignment with your social challenges is to be clear on your values.

Emotions and **T**houghts – the ET part of the PETS acronym, is typically a key focus for understanding your money personality. At first your emotions and thoughts about money may be slightly fuzzy, or alien to you. But when you learn how to notice them mindfully without negative judgments and adjust along the way, you achieve **prosperity clarity**. That's what guides your way to increased wealth and well-being.

Money Motives Matter

Our research has determined that financial behavior and decision-making is most often driven by inner motives. Motive is defined as a need or desire that causes a person to act. Your money motives, like your thoughts, can be conscious or unconscious. But since they're what drive your behavior and choices either way, they matter a great deal! It's vitally important to bring them into clear focus so you can better understand how to ease the way when adjustments are necessary for heightened financial well-being.

Think of your money motives as the heart of your **"prosperity personality."** It's what makes you tick financially and psychologically. It's important to strike a balance between both dollar sense and heart sense. The eight money motives fit common patterns we've seen in our 30 years of financial planning. The benefit in knowing your inner motivations is to help you strengthen your total prosperity – so you're in a thriving condition both inside and out.

In addition to the eight money motives, there are three processes that guide decisions. They're what can drive us **MAD** about money!

Motive – Desire that produces a specific action in seeking a certain type of outcome or result.

Avoidance – When choices are guided by moving *away* from something to avoid a negative outcome.

Drive – When choices are guided by moving *toward* something to receive a positive outcome.

In the section below, the eight money motives are identified and defined. Think about assessing each one on a scale of 0-10 to determine its degree of dominance in your financial life. The three MAD processes – Motive – Avoid – Drive – are briefly summarized for each pattern. These can be self-scored using the exercises in this book, and in using the online program, Motivated Asset Pattern Assessment (MAPA information later in the book). The money rascals identified for each motive represent the mischievous traits that can cause problems if they dominate choices too often. More information on the money rascals will be found in upcoming chapters for each money motive.

Money Motives Summary

Prestige motive:

    *is **M**otivated* by desire for social esteem or distinction, tends to ***A**void* mediocrity...

    which ***D**rives* achievement orientation & affluent lifestyles,

    creating mischief when overly dominant with *flashy* materialism ***(Flasher rascal)***

Spontaneity motive:

    *is **M**otivated* by desire for freedom from constraint, tends to ***A**void* discipline...

    which ***D**rives* creative ideas & impulsivity,

    creating mischief when overly dominant with *rash* decisions ***(Rasher rascal)***

Peace motive:
is *Motivated* by desire for calm harmony,
tends to *Avoid* conflict...
which *Drives* cooperative compliance &
inconsistency,
creating mischief when overly dominant with *clashing* choices *(Clasher rascal)*

Simplicity motive:
is *Motivated* by desire for uncomplicated clarity,
tends to *Avoid* details...
which *Drives* streamlined methods & procrastination,
creating mischief when overly dominant by *dashing*
through tasks *(Dasher rascal)*

Virtue motive:
is *Motivated* by desire for moral excellence,
tends to *Avoid* greed...
which *Drives* charitable inclinations & modest
lifestyles,
creating mischief when overly dominant that
bashes wealth as greed *(Basher rascal)*

Security motive:
is *Motivated* by desire for certainty and freedom
from worry,
tends to *Avoid* possibility of loss...
which *Drives* cautious contemplation, limiting choices,

creating mischief when overly dominant that causes *ashen* anxiety *(Asher rascal)*

Control motive:

*is **M**otivated* by desire for disciplined restraint,
tends to **A**void chaos...
which **D**rives consistent savings, precise recordkeeping,
creating mischief when overly dominant by constraining *cash* *(Casher rascal)*

Growth motive:

*is **M**otivated* by desire for ability to thrive,
tends to **A**void low returns...
which **D**rives high profit orientation and growth investing,
creating mischief when overly dominant by *stashing* aggressive stocks *(Stasher rascal)*

Honor a Balance

There isn't a satisfactory definition of wealth that suits – or is agreeable – to all people. Try finding a number that clearly defines wealth and you'll discover it's all over the place. Defining wealth is a little like trying to define beauty. They're both "in the eye of the beholder." As I stated earlier, my preferred definition of wealth is *"making the absolute most of your human and financial assets."*

Traditional definitions include words like rich, money, abundance, possessions, affluence, and econo-mic utility. Rarely is the word quantified by clear numbers that identify how much money equals wealth. Financial worries may vary considerably regardless of net worth. It's certainly possible to have "a wealth of worries" regardless of actual financial wealth. Worriers most definitely exist along the full spectrum of financial resources, but neither wealth nor poverty is a sure predictor of worry.

When we gain clarity about our distinctive human value regardless of money, it helps us worry less and make better use of the money we do have. It elevates our ability to strike a balance that honors our practical limitations, while aligning our genuine values with mindful life choices. Everyone is unique in this regard.

One of the goals of this book is to help you both feel better and do better with decisions about money, regardless of your financial resources. When your psychological habits elevate your well-being and alignment of financial and human assets, the result can truly enrich the world.

Before moving on, let's explore further the meaning of *well-being*. For this book, we mean the condition of being contented and happy. Think of contentment as ease of mind and an internal satisfaction. Even small improvements in this area are worthwhile.

We know mindfulness doesn't magically turn scarcity into abundance or austerity into prosperity, but when you put forth effort in attending to both, it has proven to heighten consciousness about choices, and lead to a more satisfying life experience.

> **One of the goals of this book is to help you both *feel* better and *do* better with decisions about money, regardless of your financial resources.**

Identify to Modify

Unconscious emotions and thoughts can seem foreign to many of us initially. There are countless reasons for this. One comes from our achievement-oriented culture, which often favors denying or suppressing emotions rather than identifying and feeling them. It can be difficult to recognize what drives our own behavior, choices, and habitual responses.

Bringing inner motives into conscious, focused awareness is the first step in taking mindful and attentive actions to create greater wealth and well-being. It's an important alignment tool to help you honor your financial and human assets. Remember, motive is neither good nor bad. It simply means desire to act in a certain way.

Here's a way to introduce new degrees of psychological awareness for yourself. Identify your most frequent feelings, thoughts, or desires (motives) when engaging in common financial activities. When you identify these mindfully, you begin to gain insight into your motivational patterns. These are at the "heart" of your money-being, but they can be modified to keep that heart ticking for good – creating both good and lasting positive results. From there, you can move into how to modify actions to gain improved outcomes that honor both wealth and well-being.

The sample dialog below is an example of an "identify to modify" conversation. You can learn to engage in similar therapeutic self-talk to gain new insights. Think of it as an interview with yourself.

Sample Dialog

Interviewer: *"How would you describe your most common feelings and thoughts when you're engaged in the task of bill paying?"*

You: *"I usually feel hurried and annoyed. Sometimes, I'm mad at myself about spending. Then I think, ok... get this under control next time around."*

Interviewer: *"Hmmm. And when the next time around comes?"*

You: *"Nothing much has changed. I must just expect it to be this way."*

Interviewer: *"So, you've identified this part of your financial experience as annoying, yet you feel a bit powerless to change it, is that correct? When you were growing up, did you ever observe others who seemed similarly annoyed or angry?"*

You: *"As a matter of fact, yes. My mother paid the bills but her anger about spending seemed directed at my father."*

Interviewer: *"So that's a bit familiar to you. Could it be that part of you has an internal expectation that money is always annoying, regardless of who's doing the spending or bill paying?"*

You: *"Interesting. That rings true. Does that mean I'm stuck with this cycle?"*

Interviewer: *"That's a great question. You're not stuck with it at all. The good news is you're already beginning to modify it, just by becoming aware of it. The next step is in identifying whether you're ready to get out of that cycle. Do you want to modify your expectation of annoyance, or are you okay with keeping this as it is?"*

You: *"I'd like to be able to pay bills and feel at least neutral or satisfied. Maybe there's part of me that's oddly at ease with the familiarity of that feeling of annoyance."*

Interviewer: *"You're really onto something here. You've just identified the secondary payoff you may get from being annoyed and mad. It's the comfort of the familiar. In the future, what's your preference – feeling annoyed or feeling satisfied?"*

You: *"Well, I'd really be an odd duck if I chose annoyance over satisfaction, wouldn't I? I think I'm ready to go for satisfaction! I might strangely miss being annoyed, but I think I'm ready to reward myself with feeling satisfied for a change."*

As you can see by the above sample dialog, the awareness of an inner dimension of financial habits is elevated. There was no criticism or defensiveness. When you invite yourself to be open to change and see it as a positive step, it's more likely to begin. You can remove the alien aspect of emotions and thoughts about money and have a genuine exploration that is brief but rich with discovery and insight.

Identify emotions and thoughts to help you modify your behavior. Remember, the motivations that matter are those that matter to you. You must *identify* what you genuinely desire as an outcome before you can *modify* habitual behaviors needed to achieve the results you want.

Embrace a more holistic and personalized definition of *wealth and well-being*. For efficiency, we suggest you use the word prosperity, as it encompasses both psychological and economic well-being.

> **Identify emotions and thoughts to help you modify your behavior.**

3

Reconstruction Zone

The money motive patterns all encourage you to assess whether you need to rebalance your existing tendencies to improve your wealth and well-being outcomes. Keep in mind, balance does not mean everything is in equal numbers or weighted identically.

Think instead of financial balance as a customized recipe for every individual, with the ingredients varying depending on your unique circumstances. Imagine how unpleasant any recipe would be if equal ingredients were used. A cup of everything, from salt and flour to every other ingredient in a muffin, for example, would create a baked item of some kind, but it certainly wouldn't be a baked *good!* One definition of balance is "a steady state." When you're in a state of well-being, you feel stable and firmly supported, not lopsided or irregular. That's what offers you the ability to function in a uniform and dependable manner. That's the goal of the mindful money process.

None of the individual money motives or their rascals are superior or inferior, right or wrong, good or bad. They all have strength areas and challenge areas. Even strengths can be problematic if they always dominate every decision. It's the classic "too much of a good thing." The money rascals (mischievous habits that can create financial problems) invite you into a lighter touch in confronting problems that can feel heavy. The money motives bring you fresh perspectives that help you balance your decisions.

Here's a simple example of "too much of a good thing." Strengths of the control motive are organization and discipline. These healthy traits drive behaviors that create systematic structure and positive savings habits.

But what if perfectionism drives the desired structure? This may require excessive time that eliminates the possibility of doing enjoyable activities. Or what if the savings habits are rigid to the point of refusing to spend for some pleasure in present day living? These are the key questions to explore in your mindful process.

The money motives provide a non-threatening springboard about whether there's a need to honor a new balance in your habits with money. We've all constructed many systems throughout our lives. Rarely is a full demolition necessary to create sufficient remodels of our money lives. But we do need to look through a new lens to fully view what we've constructed along the way, and begin to reconstruct the areas in need.

> **The money motives provide a non-threatening springboard about whether there's a need to honor a new balance in your habits with money.**

Reconstruction Zone Guide

To help you make the most of your current life circumstances, typically a few adjustments are needed. That's what happens in the reconstruction zone. It's not easy work because change can feel very disorienting. It's challenging even when you're highly motivated to modify behavior and you've identified in what new direction you want to move. Old habits can have a persistent tug, attempting to lure you into returning to your familiar comfort zone.

That's when a mentoring guide through the reconstruction zone can make all the difference. It can prevent relapsing into old patterns and empower forging ahead with the newly identified ones. At every stage and age, we're all simultaneously in a construction zone – and a reconstruction zone. We've built careers, families, relationships, and so on. We're perpetually "under construction" throughout life. Who hasn't had to adapt to reality, however, by recognizing a need to correct some aspects of what's been built previously? We must reconstruct to successfully adapt to the changes around us as our lives transition into different stages.

Under Reconstruction

As you move through your reconstruction zone, you'll assess your model in three areas:

- Emotions
- Thoughts
- Actions

Emotions, thoughts, and actions are often on unconscious "auto pilot" and have become habitual. The first step is in finding a way to notice your habits. For many people, the initial insight is in realizing that habits exist beyond behavioral ones – they exist in your mental and emotional tendencies as well. While this may seem an unfamiliar concept initially, it becomes the conveyor of hope when engaging in the work of change.

Using the money motives as the framework for assessing the three reconstruction areas, you'll build awareness and move toward attentiveness.

Emotions

In upcoming chapters, a "Top 10" list of emotional drivers is revealed for each of the money motives. When any of them are overly dominant (scores of eight or above), they can be highly intensive and seem contradictory or incompatible. This intensity drives behavioral choices that can create financial problems when acted upon too frequently. That's when it's worthwhile to enter the reconstruction zone for habitual emotions that have become problematic. It is up to you to decide whether any emotion is problematic; it's your motivation that matters.

The spontaneity motive, for example, commonly reports feeling both weakened and strengthened. How can that be? People with this motive may feel temporarily strengthened when engaging carefree choices, yet grow weary when they experience the consequences. Both emotions genuinely exist, but they reside on different sides of the emotional coin. They represent the behavioral process of simultaneously steering toward one thing while steering away from another. In this case, actions are motivated to move away from a feeling of restriction and toward a feeling of freedom.

> **The benefit in identifying emotional drivers is to help you effectively witness your own sequential patterns.**

Recognizing the consequences of problematic habits empowers insights that help you reconstruct and resolve previously stubborn dilemmas. Identify *what* emotions you experience relative to specific money matters, and *when* circumstances trigger those feelings. Then pay attention to *how* you respond during those circumstances to reveal the pattern that tends to play out repeatedly.

The benefit in identifying emotional drivers is to help you effectively witness your own sequential patterns. You'll see what triggers your reactions so that alternate actions can be suggested and practiced. It can also spur ideas for reconstructing what has historically happened for you. Proactive planning can eliminate the negative triggers altogether. This alters the sequence, making desired modifications easier to implement.

Positive emotions result from honoring a balance with money motive traits. Keep in mind, negative emotions are usually the result of an imbalance of habits. It's helpful to recognize both painful and joyful feelings, but the objective is to take intentional steps to transform negative into positive feelings. It's about consciously moving in the direction that elevates mental health. When a painful emotion is found, identify its opposite and aim for that joyful feeling as a goal for your financial well-being.

Examples of emotional transformations:

- Discouraged to Encouraged
- Worried to Relieved
- Confused to Clear
- Inadequate to Competent
- Powerless to Empowered
- Insecure to Confident

Thoughts

Generally, thoughts that are candidates for anyone's reconstruction zone are those that contain cognitive distortions. There are many forms of distorted thoughts, but the simplest way to "catch" them is to notice extremes. "All-or-Nothing" thinking captures many types of specific cognitive distortions. It becomes easier to notice them if you know what to look for. These distorted extremes typically contain words such as: always, never, all, or nothing. Here are a few examples of distorted money thoughts, with the extreme words italicized:

- "I'll *never* be able to save enough money, so I just spend it *all.*"
- "I'm the *worst* person with money on the planet. I gave up a long time ago."
- "I'm afraid *all* my money is going to disappear. It's prudent to worry *endlessly.*"

Remember, thoughts can reside in either our conscious or our unconscious awareness. Several of our thoughts are buried in our unconscious minds, yet steer our actions in many of our endeavors. It takes intentional effort to flush out the distortions and repeatedly think in a more balanced way. The three examples above could yield better well-being with the following reconstructions:

- I save enough money and spend responsibly.
- I'm capable with money and persevere with positive practices.
- I manage my emotions about money. I plan rather than worry.

Visualize Your Family Tree

Many insights can emerge from visualizing your family tree. To help discover some of your deeper beliefs about money, ask yourself if you have any rules you follow in your financial life. There may be some distortions in your examples. As you look at the branches of the people who raised you, review some general questions about your childhood. This can help ease you into significant self-discovery:

- What was the money atmosphere like when you were growing up?
- How would you describe the money habits of the people who raised you?
- Did you notice any extremes in how they seemed to think about, or act with money?

- Can you recall any specific examples of that? What meaning might you have given it at the time?
- Now think about yourself. Are you like your childhood models to any degree?
- Would you like to be more that way, less that way, or about the same as you are now?

The last question can bring remarkable insights and motivate you to make changes. The above questions help you ease into what I call the **4Ms** - **M**emories, **M**eanings, **M**ovement and **M**indfulness with money. By pondering who your money management models were growing up, your flow of thinking can move non-defensively into the meanings they may have had for you. The meanings you gave them, whether conscious or unconscious, reveal what your conclusions were at the time, which automatically guided your behavior (movement).

Often you may find your earlier behaviors were appropriate – even necessary to navigate safely – in a different period of your life. But now you may discover those behaviors are no longer necessary or helpful. They may even be sabotaging your goals. This becomes a significant insight that lifts interior obstacles that have been in your way.

The 4Ms conclude with *Mindful* reconstruction of thoughts that accurately reflect present reality. Remember, mindfulness means being aware and attentive.

> **By pondering who your money management models were growing up, your flow of thinking can move non-defensively into the meanings they may have had for you.**

You can reconstruct your previous thoughts by removing any of the extreme or inaccurate elements they may contain. Sometimes reconstruction may have to start with replacing an "absolute" word (such as never) to a "possibility" word (such as maybe). Here's a simple example:

- Change from the thought: "I'll *never* be able to save *any* money."
- To this Mindful thought: "I'm **aware** I might be able to save some money to make a worthwhile difference. I'll **attend** to this by exploring my options and choosing a savings plan."

Actions

Your discoveries from doing the 4M process (Memories, Meanings, Movement, Mindfulness) make the reconstruction zone of actions advance more smoothly, comfortably, efficiently, and effectively.

When any distortions or outdated beliefs have been removed, you feel more open to explore realistic options that will begin to provide new solutions. It doesn't magically or instantly erase all problems, but it helps ease the way to choices that build positive constructions instead of tearing down all possibilities.

Karen's 4M Example

Karen described the financial atmosphere in her home growing up as, "a bit tense." She didn't know much about how her parents managed their money, but she did remember hearing her father say on many occasions, "There's never enough money." This was the first time she realized that she'd taken on the same belief, which helped her understand where her habit of worrying about running out of money came from.

Karen's personal financial situation was stable and she was saving adequately according to her financial plan, but her worry had left her mystified and uncomfortable. Karen wanted to be less of a worrier and feel more confident. When she realized her tendency to worry was a mental habit she'd acquired from her father's example, she was able to release it and continue her planning with greater peace of mind. Her financial plan helped her stay reassured that she did have enough money.

4

8 Therapeutic Acronyms

In each upcoming money motives chapter, a case story will be presented to demonstrate how to pursue personal growth and self-awareness with therapeutic thinking. The examples represent a slice of common financial issues; none of them based on a real person. They're all composite fictional characters designed to show how the money motives commonly play out in real life, and how you can discover important growth by thinking through your answers to the questions posed in each case.

Therapeutic means to have a healthy restorative effect, designed to relieve cognitive or emotional difficulty, distress, obstacles, indecision, or mis-direction. The primary benefit of integrating therapeutic questioning into your own personal growth, is increased comfort and effectiveness in your financial planning journey. In addition, it is a tremendous courage-builder as you work at adjusting your plans. It's an important tool, also, for combatting overload when the quantity of topics would otherwise cause a sense of being overwhelmed. Think of this as therapeutic communication with yourself!

We all must work with the realities of limited time, limited financial resources, and limited readiness for change. The therapeutic growth techniques in this chapter originate from a few of my personal favorites that have been tailored for financial insights. There are several factors that make them favorites:

- They are flexible in how they can apply to any topic.
- They're designed to be easy to remember and revisit throughout life.
- They create an attitude of adventure, rather than reluctance.
- They elicit valuable information that help guide your use of professional services.
- They help you gain insights and activate positive change.

> **We must all work with the realities of limited time, limited financial resources, and limited readiness for change.**

Acronym Alert! The therapeutic acronyms I developed were purposefully designed to assist your recollection of an important concept to use in your life planning. Most of them have at least two significant meanings that reinforce each other. They create a visual image along with clear action steps and purpose. Memory training courses teach that we remember things better if they're unique and visual. That's the benefit of allowing your mind to be open to using these acronyms.

When you give them a try, you may find multiple opportunities to use them and discover they bring you significant insights on many subjects, even ones beyond money matters. They're even more empower-ing when you write out your responses.

1. AHA: Action Honoring Awareness

The AHA process helps you gain awareness of issues that need attention. It's great to have an exciting insight – or 'Aha' – but without action to alleviate problem areas, awareness alone leaves the work unfinished, and the benefits unrealized.

Use **AHA** for a double benefit of the work you're doing for your well-being:

- *Awareness* is heightened and reinforced
- *Action* is defined and acted on to honor the awareness gained

Here's how to use the **AHA** acronym process. Formulate and write down new awareness of an unconscious, unhelpful rule you've been obeying without realizing it. Reconstruct the old rule to your new, helpful, accurate one. Repeat the new rules several times a day. Our brains need the repetition to form new neural pathways.

My example of the AHA process: When I was about 10, my dad told me several financial details about the house into which we were about to move. It was unusual for him to discuss such things with me, but he seemed very matter-of-fact in his delivery of the information. It was rare to have a one-on-one experience with Dad, given our large family. Some memories are retained more vividly if they contain unusual elements, which was true for me in this example.

The day after this conversation, while riding along with my girlfriend as Dad was driving her home, I retold the house story to her – money specifics and all. The minute she was dropped off at her house, Dad immediately scolded me, "Don't you know you're *not* supposed to talk about money?" He was extremely upset. I was surprised because I'd not realized the financials he'd told me about earlier were supposed to be confidential. I felt horribly stupid and ashamed.

This vividly taught me the rule, "Don't talk about money." But as children's brains tend to do, mine created an additional all-or-nothing rigidity to it, making it distorted and unhelpful. In my mind, the rule was, "Never talk about money with anyone, or you'll get into big trouble!" Of course, I wasn't consciously aware that I'd internalized that rule until many years later.

Awareness **of previously unconscious rule:** The unconscious conclusion and rule I'd formulated in childhood caused me to feel it was wrong to discuss any finances with anyone. Obedience to that rule meant I should figure everything out for myself. So, as a young adult, I attempted to manage money well without talking to anyone about it. While certain aspects of my finances were well managed, others were unattended. There came a time when I realized this rule was mistaken, and it was time to construct a new and improved one.

Awareness **of new helpful rule:** "I'm intelligent and competent in money matters (not stupid – which was what I'd wrongly concluded from the incident). It is smart to talk about money with the right people rather than believing it's a secret that must be kept hidden."

Honoring **new awareness:** My commitment was to be aware and attentive in healthy ways about money. To fulfill and honor this commitment, the next step was to identify beliefs that had steered me toward unhelpful choices (stemming from the fear of talking about money). Then I identified my actions that had been tied to those old beliefs (being silent and passive about money). Next I reconstructed new action goals to align with my "new and improved" beliefs.

Action **(that honors awareness):** I hire professionals to assist with the many areas of prudent financial management. This was both the new rule and the new action I constructed as a young adult. It's also what attracted me to becoming a therapeutic financial planner.

Additional perspective: As an adult processing this memory therapeutically, I could easily gain a new understanding of my father's emotions about having to move into a more affordable home. He'd been very proud of the larger home we'd lived in previously. But it had proven to be financially unmanageable. This undoubtedly caused him tremendous stress and frustration. His anger while scolding me was more about his personal financial stress, rather than what I'd interpreted it to mean at the time. I was not stupid or bad, as I'd incorrectly concluded from his scolding.

It's about *Aim*, Not *Blame*: When we practice using mindful processing of our own life experiences, we're likely to find both pleasant and painful circumstances. Especially in processing difficult memories, keep "Aim" as your focus rather than "Blame." The purpose of therapeutic processing is to understand the impact an event had on the direction in which we moved. We may need to work through forgiveness of wrongs. Keep moving positively forward and never stay stuck in blame as an excuse for rejecting change. Instead, we use our fresh self-discovery to adjust our aim. Then take our first steps to move in a new direction. Continue the process and adjust our aim as we move through the circumstances of our lives.

Don't Condone, De-throne: Most of us have at one time or another allowed a distorted message to misguide us. Once we become aware of it, we must stop allowing its negative influence in our thoughts, feelings, and decisions. One of the most effective reminders is a visual image. We must knock that negative message off its throne so it can no longer "rule" us. Use this motto every time unhelpful thoughts or habits try to regain their power or sabotage your new, healthy ones: "Don't condone it, dethrone it!"

Stress: Most people have difficulty functioning optimally when stress is chronically elevated. We live in a fast-paced culture that provides an abundance of stressors. It's important to understand what your primary stressors are. These factors influence everything from your communication styles to your financial functioning.

> **Use this motto every time unhelpful thoughts or habits try to regain their power or sabotage your new, healthy ones:**
>
> **"Don't condone it, dethrone it!"**

Self-compassion reminder: It's vital to build in reminders that extend compassion to yourself for any mistakes you've identified. Mistakes are not made intentionally! As with the example above, they're often tied to misinterpretations of events that happened before you had the intellectual capacity to reach more accurate conclusions.

What matters most is learning from your mistakes, so you can prevent repeating them. Be compassionate to yourself in the process. I invite you to incorporate any of the words below to help you gain and maintain self-compassion in your process.

- Care
- Concern
- Sensitivity
- Warmth
- Mercy
- Honor
- Respect
- Understanding
- Forgiveness
- Encouragement
- Tolerance
- Kindness
- Tenderness
- Love
- Charity
- Compassion

Compassion is the prescription to alleviate ruminating regrets more commonly known as, "beating yourself up." Imagine extending the same tenderness to yourself that you'd extend to a beloved child or pet.

2. ACE: Ask – Confirm – Encourage

Ace means one that excels. Get good at practicing the three steps of **ACE** and you'll be a therapeutic communication ace! These three actions consistently net positive connections and results, whether you're asking questions of yourself for personal reflection, or using the ACE steps in conversation. Either way, with ACE, you *Ask* a question knowing you have a responsibility to listen actively to the response (even if it's listening to yourself!), so that you can accurately *Confirm* back your understanding of it. Sometimes when you're in the process of confirming, you'll naturally clarify also.

It's therapeutically beneficial to *Encourage* yourself to make meaningful connections from your life experiences and begin adjusting as needed. Encourage means to inspire with courage. Encouragement happens when we're reminded of our strengths, resources, and support as we navigate through transitions.

My example of the ACE process: In the AHA section above, I relayed a story that caused me to believe it was wrong to talk about money with anyone. It was relatively simple to see the error in that conclusion, and rewrite a better guideline. Years ago, I used ACE, to further discover additional areas the old rule was influencing, by asking, "What else has this influenced today?" Here's a glimpse into that conversation with myself:

Ask: Has the old rule, "Don't talk about money" influenced your work, and if so, in what ways?

Answer: Yes. It explains why I felt so anxious when I first began working as a financial planner. I'd felt surprised and baffled by my extreme uneasiness when asking clients about their finances. After working through the story of my "don't talk about money" rule, I realized the uneasiness was due to my childlike fear of "getting in trouble" for breaking the rule. Several new rules were needed to ease my anxiety when engaging in money discussions. I constructed a primary new rule to replace the outdated one that eased my tension and gained much improved results: "It is important to discuss all relevant details of a client's money history, for development of thorough and accurate planning strategies."

Confirm: My old rule, "Don't talk about money," was creating undue anxiety when trying to do my financial planning work. I came to realize that rule had invaded my subconscious thinking while trying to converse about a client's planning needs. I constructed a new rule that resulted in more accurate data collection for better planning. This significantly eased the discomfort the old rule had created.

Encourage: Your strengths, integrity, care, counseling, and advanced planning education are what clients rely on. It would be a disservice to both of you if you tried to create plans with insufficient discussion and information.

When you pair the first two therapeutic communication tools of AHA and ACE, you've got a dynamic duo that keeps a positive momentum going. The same is true when you add the next tools, GEM and HIRE.

3. GEM: Generate Empowered Movement

A gem is something admired for its beauty or value. Below are the four steps of the GEM process, each with a GEM acronym of its own. It can be used in multiple ways and has application in all eight money motive stories of the next chapters.

The purpose of GEM is to construct a better future even though it requires a look at the past. It's similar to the AHA process, while breaking down each step further. Each GEM step can provide significant depth and increased therapeutic awareness. It also has its own reminder of a person's intrinsic, human value.

Gather Essential Memories: These are memories that stand out vividly and most likely had unconscious meanings attached to them. It's beneficial to explore their meanings in ways like the AHA technique. Start this process by reflecting on any memories that seem vivid, then write them out. Include your feelings at the time.

Gain Enlightened Meanings: Here you pinpoint the old vs. the new meanings of the memory. Explore what it would have meant to you at the time the experience was happening. Often these may have contained distortions or inaccuracies, and were outside your conscious awareness. Examples people have shared with me over the years include beliefs such as, "I'm terrible with money," or "I can't ever get it right." Old or past interpretations such as these tend to stifle growth, healthy action, and happiness.

Reconstruct new and accurate meanings that are useful and helpful in your current life. It opens action possibilities that move from stifling to stimulating. Build in reminders of the new, accurate meanings frequently. In the examples from above, the new beliefs become, "I'm good with money," and "I can get it right." The new meanings stimulate an entirely different set of more positive responses and actions.

Grow Emotional Mindfulness: The focus here is in identifying feelings that accompanied the meanings in the memory. These are what may be keeping you stuck in a recurring pattern. With this heightened awareness, strive to notice and replace the unpleasant emotions with pleasant ones that align with the newly reconstructed meanings. This reinforces the process, and helps your brain create new neural pathways that make new habits easier to keep.

Generate Empowered Movement: Armed with helpful and accurate new meanings and mindfulness, the ability to generate empowered movement is recharged. Identify new behaviors that align with the positive meanings. The story about Tasha's new rules and goals in the prestige motive chapter is an excellent example of this.

The purpose of GEM is to construct a better future even though it requires a look at the past. When you've processed a memory with GEM steps, you can think of it as a treasured "gemory!"

GEM is useful for several topic areas, not just financial ones. When you've processed your own memories using the GEM steps, they eliminate previous inaccuracies. New constructions contain cognitive alertness and a positive focus that guides new actions.

The GEM process is quite revitalizing to do. It's even more helpful when you write your responses to the GEM steps. Then, when you've processed a memory with GEM steps, you can think of it as a treasured "*gem*ory!" *Gem*ories truly become a valuable collection of positive insights, because they put the sparkle in your spirit.

4. HIRE: Halt – Inhale – Reflect – Elect

Use the acronym HIRE to help you *"hire your higher self."* It encourages redirecting habitual responses to more effective practices. Anytime you find yourself becoming intensively emotional, it is worthwhile to pursue some understanding of the intensity. By using the four steps of HIRE below, you can unravel new threads of your own life's mysteries.

Halt

- *Halt* any response when you notice your negative or painful feelings.
- Notice your typical warning signals of an emotional reaction (such as heart rate).
- Tell yourself to stop and attend to this now before it escalates further. Then, slowly:

Inhale

- *Inhale,* exhale, and focus on the softening quality of conscious breathing.
- Send yourself a mental message to release and let go of the negative.
- Relax slowly into a full exhale, directing your emotion to soften.

Reflect

- *Reflect* on whether your reaction involves old myths or inaccurate messages.
- Notice if your reaction is flowing in from any similar past experiences.
- Identify helpful resources and options you have in the present.
- Change how you see yourself in this situation (are you becoming defensive because you took something personally that wasn't intended?).
- Generate positive insights about what you want to remember from this.

Elect

- *Elect* a different action that taps wisdom and insightful possibilities here.
- Choose effective, skillful, and intentional responses.
- Find a creative way to shift your old pattern.
- Employ the best choice under all circumstances.

When you *HIRE* your best intentional self to employ these steps, you're empowered to tap into your *higher* being. This brings superior emotional management and more positive results. Talk through some examples of your own with a trusted friend or advisor.

This practice of mindfulness increases emotional intelligence and becomes your best ally in skillfully managing and processing emotions. It can be used as a significant tool in improving many categories of your life – relationships, careers, parenting, and financial management.

> **In our American culture, there are countless philosophies about what constitutes success.**

5. COOL/FOOL Rules

COOL/FOOL stands for Culture Of Origin Lessons and Family Of Origin Lessons. It's another way to examine the beliefs we may have turned into rules to live by. The previous acronyms presented have touched on ways our families may have influenced our belief systems. Let's explore how our culture may have created expectations that are not a healthy fit for us.

In our American culture, there are countless philosophies about what constitutes success. They range from a focus on financial success using income, accumulated wealth, or material displays as indicators of success, to a more human-focused measure, such as charitable giving of time or money. Wealth, like beauty, seems to be in the eye of the beholder. On one end, it's considered a positive thing, while on the other, a negative thing. It's up to each of us to develop our own definition of success to guide our choices.

The way to use the concept of COOL or FOOL rules, is to ask yourself what has influenced your outlook about money and in what ways it has guided you. Use the money motives to help flush out messages you've heard, and to what degree you embrace any of them. Then ask if they need to be modified to any degree.

For example, what is your reaction to the statement, "The one with the most toys, wins!" It was originally written as a comical comment, but when you think about it, in American culture, there seem to be many who've bought into this belief. Does this sentiment reside in you to any degree? Has it caused any excessive spending just to gain a temporary emotional lift, or a feeling of social acceptance?

These are the types of beliefs worth reviewing to **honor a balance** between your present day needs and those of your future. There are many inaccurate cultural messages out there. Don't let them define *you*. Create your own definition of success and you'll find improved peace of mind.

6. TINT: This Is Not That

Tint means to color slightly. When you notice your own reaction to something seems extreme, it may be an indicator of a warning signal that was triggered by your brain's alarm system. The problem with these alarms is they're often false ones based on past experiences that have some degree of similarity to an event that's occurring in the present. In this respect, the "false alarm" has tinted – or colored – your mood based on this biological protection system. If you suspect that's occurring with you, you can inquire by asking yourself, "Does the alarm feeling have some similarity to another event I've experienced in the past?"

If you're prone to worry or have experienced significant stress or trauma in your life, using this as a checking-in process is significantly grounding when you are anxious. Our brains are biologically designed to fire off countless alarms as a self-protective mechanism, storing all kinds of memories that build its alarm system. The problem is, many of the accumulated alarms are over-reactive or totally irrelevant to the current situation.

If you have past distressing life events, remember they may occasionally cause false alarms when anything remotely similar is encountered. Trigger examples can be a strangers' tone of voice, a facial expression, a song, or even a fragrance. This is where **TINT** comes in. TINT helps you claim and disclaim emotional triggers that do not apply to a current situation.

Check-in with your feeling, asking yourself:

- "Am I reacting to something from the past rather than this current situation?"
- "What experience might be triggering this reaction?"
- "Does this have any actual danger, or is it mostly a false alarm?"

If you determine it's mostly a false alarm, engage in therapeutic self-talk to calm your distress, using **TINT – This Is Not That.** Your self-talk would sound something like this, "Oh, this was triggered because it had a similarity to a different event and my brain is trying to protect me from that other danger. But that danger is not present here; this is not that, so I can ignore the alarm and regain calm."

For people who've been abused, victimized by crime, war, or another trauma, the TINT tool can be especially helpful. It helps you claim and then disclaim your own reaction. Or if you're a fishing enthusiast, try using "Catch and Release" as the benefit of TINT. *Catch* yourself at a false alarm, then *release* it. Since the goal is maximum well-being, it is always helpful to keep the color of our moods clear or positively tinted for good.

7. TWEDY: To What Extent Do You

TWEDY can be used to weigh what is most important to you for prioritization processing, and to what degree any topic matters to you. It can also help you gauge what adjustments you're willing or ready to make to improve many of your life planning issues.

TWEDY is a bountiful sentence stem that can frame many pertinent questions worth asking for improved self-understanding. TWEDY stands for:

To What Extent Do You

_____?

From here, complete the sentence stem by filling in the blank with just about any subject you're working on. It helps you discover how much you care about a topic, and to what extent you're ready to take some new action. A TWEDY-based question also tends to elicit more honest answers. Several examples are below.

> **Feel free to use the TWEDY concept with slight variations of the words so they have fresh inspiration for you.**

To What Extent Do You:

- Want analysis about the amount of money you need to save to fund your goals?
- Feel ready to begin taking steps to modify some of your previous habits with money?
- Care about improving how you and your spouse or partner handle money conflicts?
- Intend to provide for your child's college funding needs?
- Feel concern about your healthcare expenses at older ages?
- Want calculations done so you can compare your possible options?
- Worry about money issues?

Feel free to use the TWEDY concept with slight variations of the words so they have fresh inspiration for you. You'll become a master at discovering your true financial priorities using TWEDY. Variations include:

- To what degree are you interested in adjusting_____?
- How important is it to you to _____?
- On a scale of 1-10, how important is it to you to resolve _____?
- How high a priority is it to you to _____?
- What is your willingness to get this resolved?
- How much do you care about _____?
- Describe how intensely you feel about _____.

- To what extent do you feel ready to start making modifications in_____?

When you combine your honest self-assessment skill with your authentic motivations, then positive action is much more likely to be gained and maintained. TWEDY is therapeutic because of the understanding and awareness it creates.

8. NEAR: Numb–Emotional–Adjusting–Rebuilding

NEAR is the acronym I created to help people who are grieving a significant loss. Transitions can be small or large. The number of changes they necessitate varies considerably. They may range from excruciating to just mildly difficult. For significant losses, such as the death of a close loved one, divorce, unemployment, or a health crisis, grief with intense emotions is the natural response. It is unique in that you can't "achieve your way out of it."

The NEAR acronym can help you gain awareness of the common stages or elements of grief. These aren't strictly progressive stages, but they generally follow this order. Keep in mind that these elements sway back and forth, almost like tree branches in a strong wind.

1. **N**umb – is typically the initial response to the news of a loss, even if it was expected. The shock may be understood intellectually, but emotionally and physically there is numbness that blocks

out some of the feelings that come later. It is a protective experience that releases slowly.

2. **E**motional – there are multiple emotions that grieving people experience. No two are the same and the length of time varies. Common emotions include feeling fearful, anxious, sad, depressed, confused, angry, apathetic, lonely, or conflicted.

3. **A**djusting – After several weeks or months, some of the intensity of emotions diminishes and a period of adjustment is experienced. There may or may not be a feeling of acceptance of the loss, but there is a degree of adapting to changes brought on by the loss.

4. **R**ebuilding – Much of the earlier stages are focused on the past and coping with the present. Rebuilding is evidenced by a renewed interest in the future, with an interest and ability to make plans.

Don't hesitate to engage additional support via mental health professionals who specialize in grief when you experience loss. You'll also find comfort in the book *Rays of Hope in Times of Loss – Courage and Comfort for Grieving Hearts*.

5

Money Motive #1
Prestige

Prestige Summarized: The prestige pattern is *motivated* by achievement and a quality of life that provides perceived freedom to spend on upscale items and have success recognized. This may lead you to *avoid* mediocrity – anything perceived to be of poor quality or image. If overly dominant, it may *drive* a pattern of *"flashy"* spending that leads to debt, stress, and the eventual loss of adequate financial resources needed for future necessities.

Prestige Strengths: Prestige has a strong internal achievement orientation that commonly drives higher incomes that can bring material pleasures and other benefits. This positive focus for success may be coupled with discovering social and other lifestyle comforts that gratify the prestige pattern. Most likely, you have a pleasing personality with a flair for generous hosting or gifting to others. Frequently both entertaining and entertained by your income success, you've acquired a keen sense of product quality for upscale living.

Recognition for your achievement and success is likely important to you. Pursuit of status or image can have a positive energizing element as a strength. It's important to maintain balance in this pursuit, so that affluent lifestyle expenses are managed to allow for adequate savings to fund future needs.

Prestige Rascal/Challenge Areas: *Flasher* is the rascal personality named for the money mischief that can happen in the prestige motive, due to your flair for *flashy* spending on image items. This is not a problem, in and of itself, but it may cause an avoidance of saving. The positive aspects of the flasher style are an energetic enjoyment of life's pleasures and social enthusiasm that often bring delight to others.

Dominance in this style may be challenged by an internal dialog driving a desire to build a feeling of success by displaying it externally. If spending becomes excessive and causes debt or insufficient savings, the emotional consequence is the opposite of what you seek. To preserve prestige, honoring reasonable current spending and future savings helps achieve improved financial outcomes along with more positive emotions.

Flasher's Rhyme

*Look here, I'm **Flasher** and I'm one cool cat.*
I am the one you should want to look at!
My toys are flashy, take lots of cashy—
Without them I'm afraid I might feel trashy!
When I show off I feel a little better,
Even if that makes me a major debtor!

Emotional Drivers of Dominant Prestige Motive:

_ Superior
_ Inferior
_ Proud
_ Guilty
_ Powerful
_ Powerless
_ Deserving
_ Inadequate
_ Isolated
_ Connected

Look closely at the "Top 10" list of emotional drivers in the prestige motive. Notice the appearance of contradiction in this pattern's emotions, such as "superior" and "inferior." What's going on when prestige drives all actions? Let's look at the first pair of emotions as an example. They aren't as contradictory as they first appear.

Actions are often motivated by an attempt to move toward a feeling of superiority and move away from, or eliminate a feeling of inferiority. It's an inner game with any emotionally-driven behavior. A dominant prestige motive is especially important to understand because it may have some deep or hidden insecurity driving it. When external images have become a requirement for feeling good about your human value, it's worthwhile to take a deeper look. Professional counselors and coaches can be an excellent resource for this. Building intrinsic self-worth helps this pattern resist the external trappings of prestige-seeking that provide only temporary and artificial relief.

> **When external images have become a requirement for feeling good about your human value, it's worthwhile to take a deeper look.**

Prestige Motive Rebalance: Although the prestige pattern has a strong achievement orientation and ambition for success, finding balance by expanding the definition of success is a helpful strategy. Prestige is often the underlying reason for significant lifestyle expenditures. Material purchases may have become an unconscious expectation to reward success. Rarely has it been quantified over time. It may be disguised as good taste or necessary for continued success in occupational pursuits.

Discover how you measure success for yourself. Use TWEDY (To What Extent Do You...) to further assess the degree to which you feel you seek external validation as a measure of your value. For example, to what extent do you feel unsuccessful or overlooked if you're not receiving recognition for your achievements? If this is highly true for you, it's worth an effortful rebalance so you can build up your internal prestige – your pure value as a human being. List your human assets – your unique and positive traits – so you can begin to embrace those more frequently.

Identify what makes you feel genuinely valuable and gratified, regardless of social group definitions. Review unconscious expectations you may have had, and construct updated ones that align with your current wisdom and values.

If you've noted prestige-oriented spending issues, the best thing to do is acknowledge the desire that underlies the behavior. Then, aim to **honor a balance** so your future finances are strengthened and not sabotaged by an overabundance of current prestige spending. The challenge areas here can be extensive and deeply embedded, so it's useful to flush out underlying thoughts and emotions that may be causing repetitive choices and problems. Persistently pursue truth by asking yourself the degree to which you're willing to practice adjusting your past habits, to create better results in the future.

Honoring Mindful Prestige Strategies: It's vital to grow your inner sense of worth and not tie yourself exclusively to external achievements. The more you enjoy spending, the more important it is to put financial systems in place that attend to funding future needs. That way, you'll have funds available throughout your life. Create automatic savings and investment plans that go directly into accounts you'll need for various purposes.

Your desire for prestige will be part of your personality even as an older person, so it's important that money is consistently set aside for those years. You don't want to be emotionally drained later in life due to insufficient funds. If external displays of success are creating money problems, continue examining your belief systems about self-worth, so you aren't dependent on material displays to feel internally valuable as a person.

A Case Example of Prestige: Tara was a successful marketing manager who'd worked hard to earn her MBA. She'd started as a project assistant and rapidly was promoted to manager. With each promotion, her salary increased substantially and she felt successful, as she put it, "on the outside." But on the inside, she reported feeling inadequate, empty, and anxious. Although she earned more than enough money to support a comfortable lifestyle, her spending began to exceed her earnings.

Tara said she especially noticed anxiety after her most recent promotion, when her higher income exceeded her father's at the height of his career. She dismissed the feeling and continued to purchase items that gave her a temporary feeling of relief. It was never long before she felt the pang of inadequacy again, and she'd find herself shopping for new clothes and jewelry to feed her need to look successful. Her credit card debt was growing and she wasn't keeping up with payments. Tara did the Motivated Asset Pattern Assessment (MAPA) exercise, and her top three money motive scores were (range 0-10):

Prestige – 9
Spontaneity – 9
Peace – 7

Tara began her mindful money process with the **ACE (Ask – Confirm – Encourage)** therapeutic communication steps. She *Asked* herself when she'd lost the ability to keep up with her spending. Tara found that, paradoxically, she'd kept up well when she had a lower salary. However, with each incremental salary increase and promotion, her "urge to splurge" not only happened more frequently, but with greater intensity. While pondering her spending history, she realized that it was when her salary exceeded her father's that she stopped keeping track of her credit card charges. That's also when she experienced what she called a "double whammy" of doubly intense empty, anxious feelings that she coped with by spending more.

Tara *Confirmed* that she had a positive cash flow until her latest promotion when her earnings exceeded those of her father. Tara further explored her use of the word, "empty," to describe her feeling. She realized she was doing a shopping version of consuming empty calories, but in her case, it was empty spending. This meant some purchases were not genuinely needed nor were they good for her financial health. She confirmed they'd filled her empty feeling, but it never lasted.

Tara reminded herself of past successes to gain *Encouragement*. She'd kept up with expenses and never carried any credit card debt when she earned less money. She acknowledged her ability to manage her money successfully, adding that she had excellent organizational skill.

Tara also used the 4M process (Memories, Meanings, Movement, Mindfulness) to better understand why her elevated earnings may have caused anxiety. One of her money memories was about her father's frequent statements about earning more than her mother. As Tara reflected on the meaning she'd given it, she realized her subconscious conclusion had become "girls should earn less than boys."

This became a "rule to live by" for Tara, which she unconsciously obeyed by artificially creating a lower income by spending too much. Her father had been her first model of measuring human value with financial earnings tied to gender expectations. Tara felt significant liberation in modifying her previously unconscious expectation and changing her self-imposed earnings limitation rule.

Tara created several new rules and goals to honor herself *and* her financial plan:

- Pay off my credit card balances
- Add no new credit card debt
- Use cash for spending and follow pre-set limits
- Enroll in my company's 401K plan and maximize the employer match
- Increase my 401K savings when my debt is paid off
- Write positive affirmations of my human assets to honor myself and my plan
- Create a list of alternate behaviors other than shopping when I feel empty or anxious
- Identify two friends I can call if I'm tempted to do "empty spending"
- See a therapist for additional help if my feelings of anxiety return

Tara sees a financial practitioner now as well, to review her progress and get technical advice about her investments, tax strategies, and other future planning questions. Working together with professionals has helped her honor her wealth and well-being. Tara reports, "I still get that urge to splurge sometimes, but now I'm able to honor myself by shifting gears when that happens and choose an activity that feeds both my plan and my self-worth. Good planning also allows for a few splurges that are high priority to me."

6

Money Motive #2
Spontaneity

Spontaneity Summarized: The spontaneity pattern is *motivated* by being free from feeling constrained or deprived. Decisions tend to be *"rash"* or impulsive. Natural at embracing pleasure and living for the moment, this style may *avoid* internalizing the benefits of longer-term savings. This tends to *drive* an imbalance of impulse purchases or a lack of discipline in other money management decisions. If loss or debt occurs, it can cause a feeling of discouragement that perpetuates the cycle rather than making needed adjustments.

Spontaneity Strengths: What an excellent and creative resource this pattern can be for recognizing and acting on many enjoyable and fun products and activities! Spontaneity drives people to be open to new ideas and opportunities. You have a positive influence socially for engaging pleasurable events. You tend to be flexible in your choices. Typically, you live for today, enjoy pleasing people, and strive to be light-hearted.

Your purchases may not have the extravagance of the prestige motive and may be relatively modest per item. Your strengths can become too much of a good thing if the frequency of your spontaneous decisions grow debt instead of stability. Your flexibility with the right guidance can help you strive to drive toward the benefits of balance, so you can enjoy the rewards of intentional decisions that "buy" enjoyment later in life also.

Spontaneity Rascal/Challenge Areas: *Rasher* is the rascal personality known for making *rash* or impulsive decisions. Too much impulsivity can cause you to avoid being disciplined in your spending and savings. Common consequences are growing debt, lack of savings, and disappointment in others who don't show appreciation for your efforts to please. You may also be vulnerable to investment losses if rash reactions to market fluctuations or other short-term circumstances are acted upon. This style may indicate some money management challenges due to an internal dialog that says, "Give in to emotions to feel good." To manage impulsive emotions, the key is to recognize and resist the misleading ones when they occur.

Rasher's Rhyme

*Say hi to **Rasher**, I love impulse buys,*
Right through my fingers money usually flies!
I think a budget is a mighty pest,
It takes away my fun and spending quest!
I care the most about my here and now,
Plan for the future? I would not know how!

Emotional Drivers of Dominant Spontaneity Motive:

_ Stimulated
_ Carefree
_ Burdened
_ Urgent
_ Stuck
_ Rebellious
_ Impulsive
_ Conflicted
_ Weakened
_ Strengthened

If you have a high degree of preference for spontaneity, you may relate to all "Top 10" emotional drivers. On the one hand, you are stimulated by your impulses and enjoy acting on them. On the other hand, you feel greatly displeased by some of the negative consequences in your financial life. Look at each emotional driver and ask, "What action do I take when I have this emotion? How did it turn out? How long did any positive feelings last from giving in to the impulse?" Acknowledge the "urge to splurge" and the commonality of it. The power in claiming it lies in taming it so it is acted upon less frequently.

Spontaneity Motive Rebalance: Keep strengths in mind for which you compliment yourself, such as a "going with the flow flexibility" of this pattern. Manage impulsive behavior by creating structure to prevent it. While this personality can be complimented for making quick decisions, it needs some boundaries identified to prevent debt or negligence of savings. Think of the boundaries as building freedom into your future by setting up adequate funding for your needs down the road.

> **While this personality can be complimented for making quick decisions, it needs some boundaries identified to prevent debt or negligence of savings.**

Quantify the consequences of giving in to rash decisions. Gain a sense of how frequently these types of actions have occurred in the past, and the costs that have mounted over time. It's valuable to understand this, so you can integrate the most suitable new actions into your plan.

Honoring Mindful Spontaneity Strategies: When *spontaneity* motives dominate money decisions, begin by recognizing the higher intensity of your emotional drivers. This pattern houses highly reactive energy and is often the most creative in finding frequent, interesting, and entertaining ways to spend. Build awareness that the financial consequences of acting on impulse too frequently can be severe.

It's important to attend to building systematic savings and investment systems so they aren't avoided, neglected, or sabotaged. Impulsivity can also occur with investment decisions, so it's prudent for you to have an understanding with your financial advisor that decisions will be discussed before acted upon.

Create a "Resist-it Kit" of action steps to follow instead of giving in to an impulse. This includes noting the desire and emotional urge when it hits, and putting a minimum 48-hour rule of inaction on it. Collaborate with an advisor on additional best steps to follow when the spontaneous "urge to splurge" kicks in. That's the best way to prevent an excessive expense or investment sabotage.

A Case Example of Spontaneity: Toby and Carrie became proud new parents at age 31, gleefully welcoming into their lives a baby girl, Haley. In their five years of marriage they'd noticed their outlooks about money were clashing often, but they rarely resolved their differences.

Growing up, Toby was the youngest of three children in his family. His parents' financial success had blossomed during his upbringing, which they enjoyed and freely shared with Toby. Although his two older siblings had part-time jobs in high school, Toby's parents felt proud that he didn't need a job to help pay for his social and clothing expenses. They gave him money whenever he wanted it.

Carrie was the oldest of six children. Both of her parents were frugal and disciplined in their financial decision-making. Carrie began earning income at age 13 as the neighborhood baby-sitter, then at retail stores through high school and college. She was proud that she never succumbed to the temptation to buy unneeded items simply because she got a "deal" with her employee discount. Carrie paid an agreed upon portion of her college tuition and expenses from her savings and earnings.

The day Carrie and the baby were leaving the hospital, Toby arrived with more than a car and car seat. He had a trunk full of gifts for Carrie and little Haley. Carrie felt a flash of concern about what it all cost, conscious of their reduced income during her maternity leave. But she dismissed it due to the jubilance and pride Toby displayed about his trunk full of "Treasures for my Treasures!" But several months later, Toby was still spontaneously buying multiple gifts for Haley. None of the individual items cost a great deal, but the small expenses added up to significant totals. Carrie was the household bill payer, but their income was insufficient for all of Toby's gift buying. She began to complain, but she felt powerless over his spending and uncertain of her place now that she was no longer earning income.

Toby's "treasure trips" needed a little **AHA (Action Honoring Awareness)** processing to help him gain fresh awareness of how to manage his spontaneity. While his gift giving gave him great joy, it gave the family great debt. Toby and Carrie had both agreed they wanted to have a positive cash flow, but neither had been prepared for the psychological challenges of their new life as a family.

Carrie was less assertive about Toby's spending habits due to her unexpected confusion tied to her unpaid maternity leave. Toby's desire for spontaneity grew in his exuberance over Haley, compounded by the multitude of baby items adorably displayed at his favorite retail stores. He admitted that most of his treasures were nonessential items.

Financial analysis was necessary to help them gain heightened *Awareness* of what they'd need to do to prevent debt and begin saving some money for future goals. This was helpful to both Toby and Carrie, as they now could quantify where their money should be allocated if they indeed wanted to fund their goals.

The second AHA awareness was more psychological, as it brought insightful understanding of Toby's excitement for gift-giving. When asked what money meant to his parents in relation to how they interacted with Toby, he replied, "Well, clearly, money was love to my parents. They were happy to pay for everything for me and I felt loved when they gave it to me. I can't remember exactly what they said when they gave money to me, but it was always something very affectionate. I was never made to feel guilty for receiving their money. Thinking of it this way, I must admit I have also internally felt like money and gifts demonstrate love. I just automatically thought that's how I should show my love for Carrie and Haley no matter what. This is helpful, because every time Carrie complained about my spending, I felt unloved and rejected."

For Carrie, however, money or gifts did not mean love to her. Managing money well represented love to her. Toby's excessive gifts didn't make her feel loved. If anything, they made her doubt his love, because it felt like a broken promise when Toby overspent. This was a powerful AHA insight for them both. They chose *Action* to *Honor* this *Awareness* by coming up with newly remodeled meanings for money that uniquely fit them as a couple. Carrie and Toby both wanted to modify their childhood money messages and formulate their own. Their new mindful money principle helped them honor both by building in a few enjoyable pleasures in the present, while building in savings for their future goals. This became their guiding principle for taking actions in their financial planning.

Toby's Motivated Asset Pattern Assessment (MAPA) revealed just two primary motives:

Spontaneity – 8
Peace – 6

Carrie's MAPA scores showed one primary motive with three secondary motives.

Control – 9
Virtue – 6
Peace – 6
Growth – 6

Toby and Carrie felt their money motive findings gave a useful "direction reflection." Toby indicated he wanted to focus more on their new awareness of love, money, and balance to help him lower his spontaneity score and raise his control score. Carrie's additional work is found in the Control Motive chapter.

7

Money Motive #3
Peace

Peace Summarized: This pattern is *motivated* by a desire for calm and freedom from conflict. There's often an unsettled internal conflict about money, however, due to desires or goals that *"clash"* with each other. Peace seeking usually motivates a cooperative and flexible personality style. The preference to *avoid* conflict, however, may *drive* inconsistent choices with money. This can be in several money matters: spending vs. saving; long-term vs. short-term goals; high vs. low risk tolerance; slow and consistent vs. rushed and unpredictable.

Peace Strengths: Strengths of the peace motive can be a valuable gift, as your cooperative spirit eases the way for many people in all kinds of situations. As a peace-oriented person, you are motivated to avoid conflict, and have likely developed amazing talent for keeping the peace in family and perhaps in social groups as well. You can adapt to several objectives with positive persistence, and are especially compliant when you fully understand goals. With money, you let your goals determine your direction. Being cooperative can become problematic if you receive conflicting guidance about your money, because you're not sure who to please. This upsets your peace-seeking motive because you may become self-critical due to inconsistent decisions.

Peace Rascal/Challenge Areas: *Clasher* is the rascal personality stemming from unclear, *clashing* desires or goals. Some belief systems of the clasher rascal may originate from inadequate information or the absence of healthy role models earlier in life. You may tend to switch back-and-forth in financial decisions due to conflicting opinions that come from multiple sources. With clarified goals that show funding requirements, clashers often find it effective to "talk back" to the unhelpful thoughts and emotions that may try to sabotage new, healthier behaviors. Use the positive persistence of this style in finding the right mix of professional guidance and financial analysis.

Clasher's Rhyme

*They call me **Clasher** 'cuz I fight myself,*
I can't decide if I want stuff or wealth!
I save my money for a while but then,
I take it ALL and find a way to spend!
No matter what I do, I feel a fool,
Like either way I'm breaking someone's rule!

Emotional Drivers of Dominant Peace Motive:

__ Indecisive
__ Challenged
__ Uneasy
__ Ambivalent
__ Conflicted
__ Lost
__ Regretful
__ Inconsistent
__ Fragmented
__ Unsettled

The theme of the "Top 10" Peace motive emotions is an inner unsettled feeling of perpetual indecision. You may avoid decisions altogether due to ambivalence about what is right. Because you're driven by conflict avoidance, you often second-guess the decisions you do make. If you are dominated by a desire to always "keep the peace," you may end up feeling frequently unpeaceful about how to be more consistent in your financial universe. With conflicting information, you may experience what might feel like motion sickness, as you sway back and forth, or up and down in trying to discover what is the best course of action for you.

Peace Motive Rebalance: Those who seek peace are motivated to avoid conflict. They tend to have a cooperative personality and desire to please others, which is a positive thing. If you've frequently encountered times when you've given in to something to please someone and avoid conflict, a rebalance is in order. When peace is a dominant motive, you've likely not known how to resolve potential conflicts other than giving in. Financial disharmony can be internal or external. If you have some back-and-forth confusion about financial decisions, financial analysis can be the deciding factor to help you resolve your dilemmas.

For external conflicts in relationship dynamics, a peace-motivated person appreciates finding a way to be heard without it causing an escalation of the disagreement with another person. One of the best things to consider is hiring a practitioner who can integrate this understanding into your process. That way, all parties can be heard and solutions of compromise created. The power of acknowledging differences and receiving expert advice is an excellent tiebreaker.

Honoring Mindful Peace Strategies: When *peace* motives drive decisions too heavily, emotions tend to be in a perpetually unsettled state. This is because the peace-driven goal seeker longs for reliable resolution to perceived contradictions in what financial actions are best. Peace-motivated styles will avoid conflict, but may not have adequate information and guidance to create a lasting solution. This is sometimes due to lacking financial analysis to break the tie of spending and savings decisions. Having this done on a consistent basis is a critical step to tame clashing emotions and achieving the peace you desire.

The peace pattern may indicate a thought process that misguides you due to ever-changing priorities. These range from "I should enjoy my money by spending it freely" to "I'm going to end up homeless if I don't save more." Such clashes may also result from observing opposite money styles when growing up or living in a stressful financial environment. The need for calculated strategies that are prioritized and goal-focused will ease conflicts and help create peaceful resolutions.

> **When peace motives drive decisions too heavily, emotions tend to be in a perpetually unsettled state.**

A Case Example of Peace: Ruby and Rosie are 70-year old twins who live together in a small home. Ruby had never been married but she always lived near Rosie and she adored being an aunt and great aunt to Rosie's children and grandchildren. When Rosie's husband, Ted, passed away four years earlier, she invited Ruby to live with her. They'd always gotten along well and had talked about the possibility of being "roomies" again. They would share expenses monthly. Although they were identical twins, their money lives were far from identical.

As a single woman, Ruby had worked as a teacher and lived contentedly within her means. She'd retired from teaching at age 65 with a modest pension. Ruby had also saved additional assets in a retirement account. Since she'd mastered the art of living within her means, it was most important to her that her money was predictably safe. Ruby's dominant money motive was security and her decisions reflected that.

Rosie, unlike Ruby, had never worked outside the home. Ted had earned a good living as a software engineer but they had very little savings. Early in their marriage, Rosie wanted to manage their finances to "earn her keep" as she put it. She went back and forth in her spending and savings habits, however. Rosie admitted that she often felt conflicted about her financial decisions. When Ted would occasionally voice his opinion about how they "should get into the stock market," she'd open some mutual fund accounts to keep the peace. But when the market news was bad, Rosie would panic and move the money back into money market accounts, which locked in their losses. Rosie remained mystified about what her own true preferences were. Now, as a widow, her inconsistency was starting to bother Ruby. Rosie would lose bills, pay them late, and sometimes use her credit card to borrow money to pay bills. More and more often, Rosie asked Ruby if she could borrow money from her. Ruby decided they needed professional guidance and Rosie was willing to go along.

Rosie and Ruby met with a therapist and financial practitioner who worked together to help clients resolve financial dilemmas. The therapist created a genogram (family tree chart) to gain an understanding of the people in their lives. Both Rosie and Ruby described their parents as financial opposites. Their mother was conservative and frugal. Their father always found new ways to spend their money. They argued frequently. The therapist asked each woman if she had financial traits of either parent. As you may have guessed, Rosie identified with her father and Ruby identified with her mother. Ruby's assessment is described in the Security Motive chapter.

Rosie's Motivated Asset Pattern Assessment (MAPA) profile showed three dominant motives, which explained her frequently conflicted feelings:

Peace – 8
Spontaneity – 6
Control – 6

Her highest pattern was in the peace motive, known for avoiding conflict and driving inconsistent choices. Her next two patterns were tied for second place with scores of six. One was spontaneity, the other was control. These two styles are opposites, so they have built-in conflicts. Spontaneous choices avoid discipline, which drives impulsive decisions. Control-driven motives avoid chaos and desire organization and consistent savings. Rosie was basically acting like dad one minute and mom the next. Either way, she felt like she was always displeasing someone – "like I'm breaking a rule that I can't quite see" – no matter what her financial decisions were.

Rosie shared her emotions and thoughts with both the therapist and planner. She'd been unaware how profoundly her parents' disharmony had unconsciously influenced her. Together they identified several habits Rosie had developed that she now wanted to modify. She realized it was high time to define her unique prosperity personality, so she could take actions that aligned with her true human assets. More of Ruby's story is in the security motive chapter.

8

Money Motive #4
Simplicity

Simplicity Summarized: The simplicity pattern is *motivated* by uncomplicated clarity and ease. This motive may *avoid* details often due to overloaded schedules and perception of role demands. Simplicity-motivated styles may *"dash"* through their many daily tasks. Relative to money management, this may often *drive* shortcut methods that seem to work well in the near-term, but may result in procrastination or errors over longer periods. This motive creates an impressive focus on multiple interests that compete with optimal money management.

Simplicity Strengths: Your strength is in doing multiple actions. Your busy calendar and multiple interests are impressive and you are driven to go! Even when you run out of energy, your drive finds a way to keep you going. In many ways, you are quite efficient and creative in your streamlined methods for getting more and more done. Your active schedule and diverse interests keep you energized and interesting to others. You may sometimes wonder if you'd get bored if you slowed down. Your strength may at times create a pattern of neglect for attending to the details of prudent financial management. Your streamlined methods may omit logistics that cause procrastination or missed deadlines that cost you financially. Delegating details in this area will enhance your existing strengths and prevent procrastination.

Simplicity Rascal/Challenge Areas: *Dasher* is the rascal personality of the simplicity motive. Dashers *dash* from one activity to the next, and their strength is often an impressive aptitude for getting things done. But financial tasks are avoided too frequently. This is sometimes due to a dislike or discomfort with financial matters, while for other dashers it's a natural consequence of an over-burdened schedule. Dashers who partner with a financial professional typically experience much progress due to the assistance of prioritization in planning. Automatic systems and consistent communication for staying updated are essential for this style.

Dasher's Rhyme

*My name is **Dasher** and I'm in a rush,*
If you say "plan" to me I'll tell you, "Hush!"
I'm in a hurry, no time to worry,
My thought of money is a little blurry!
I've got to go now, don't you dare say "No" now,
When I am ready, I will just say "Whoa now!"

Emotional Drivers of Dominant Simplicity Motive:

__ Rushed
__ Impatient
__ Inattentive
__ Overwhelmed
__ Distracted
__ Deprived
__ Over-extended
__ Disoriented
__ Unorganized
__ Pressured

The "Top 10" list for people motivated by simplicity shows a pattern of stress due to overloaded responsibilities and activities. Review the list and check off which emotions seem to drive your actions (or inactions). Then reflect on how you can **honor a balance** that brings more calm into your emotional life with money. The benefit of balance here can change the list from frantic to calmly manageable. Delegating certain tasks rather than ignoring them is a welcome strategy that can free you up to do remaining tasks more consistently.

Simplicity Motive Rebalance: Identify which tasks you'll delegate to professional services and which ones you can effectively complete yourself. This helps eliminate ongoing procrastination and the denial of this motive, "I'll do it tomorrow."

Those who are motivated by simplicity are often extremely busy people who need efficiency due to lack of time. You can be complimented for the multitude of tasks you manage in a typical day. With your money life, it's useful to review the shortcuts you've leaned on for getting basic functions done, and list those that have been neglected. Then create new balance by delegating some functions to financial professionals who have systems they can implement with your guidance.

It's also useful to determine if the neglected matters in your finances are due to a lack of time, or if they're due to a lack of interest in doing certain financial tasks. You may also uncover a sense of discomfort due to inexperience as the reason for avoiding financial management. Ask yourself, "What underlies my unattended areas?" Your responses will guide you to seek the proper assistance for getting needed tasks more fully completed. It may also be helpful to estimate the cost and consequences of neglecting financial tasks. That can be motivational.

> **Those who are motivated by simplicity are often extremely busy people who need efficiency due to lack of time.**

Honoring Mindful Simplicity Strategies: When *simplicity* motives drive behavior, financial details may be neglected entirely. To honor this motive while improving your financial plan results, participate in employer-sponsored retirement plans or other automatic savings. Pay attention to additional costs that erode your savings potential due to late fees with bill-paying, higher interest costs from poor credit ratings, or high prices paid when no price comparisons are made.

If your "To Do" list is unmanageable, the first step is to acknowledge that fact. The second step is to consider curtailing some of your activities. Engage professional expertise to help you prioritize and organize. Delegation of financial and organizational tasks such as bill paying and investment allocation management is critical to solving problems of procrastination and neglect.

A Case Example of Simplicity: Mary and Todd have been married for 20 years. They're happy, active empty nesters with doctorates in Organizational Development and a thriving consulting business. They struggled to make ends meet in the early years of their business, and any extra money was reinvested in the firm to improve technology and marketing. They reasoned this was the best investment they could make. However, they decided to find out more about retirement planning when they both turned 50.

Mary and Todd's money motives were assessed and used to structure a conversation about their historic style and preference in financial matters. Their practitioner introduced the exercise, adding that it helps people when they "identify to modify" any desires, goals, or habits they'd like to address. Mary and Todd exhibited nearly identical dominant motives, which reflected the busy, achievement-oriented lives they'd spent together. Their schedules had always been demanding and full, which they said energized them. Their top two motivated asset patterns were **(range 0–10):**

    Simplicity – 9
    Growth – 9

They considered their business to be their retirement plan. Their only savings was an interest-bearing money market account, established for emergencies or cash flow shortages in the business. They'd not assessed the market value of their business, but they felt optimistic about selling it when they were ready to retire. As attentive as Mary and Todd had been about growing their business, they'd been inattentive about their retirement funding. They'd kept it too simple. Their desire for simplicity had unconsciously created a lopsided financial picture.

Mary and Todd had similar upbringings. Both sets of their parents had uncomplicated lives and never discussed money openly. They had worked in stable jobs and lived on pension incomes that adequately met their needs. Mary and Todd described each parent's financial outlook and habits as follows:

Mary's Descriptions:

Mom was *quiet* about money. She seemed *calm* and *optimistic.* Mom wasn't very happy with her job, and I remember she advised me once to do work that I found personally rewarding. Mom said she chose to stay with her employer because of the *pension benefit* which would keep her retirement plan *simple.*

Dad seemed to have a greater pride in his work and the income it provided. He said he felt *entrepreneurial* in his role because he had significant *financial power.* His compensation was tied to the *growth* of the company, and he often said it kept his *pension funded* nicely, too.

Todd's Descriptions:

My father was an *academic*. He was especially focused on his research and said he had *no time* to *complicate* things with thinking about money. He knew his retirement funding was *'built in'* to the deal as he put it, and that suited him perfectly. The only time he was ever in a bad mood about money was when he prepared their tax returns. He just *hated messing with it."*

My mother never worked outside the home, but she was the family's *bookkeeper*. She seemed to be a natural at keeping it *organized*, suggesting that was the key to *keeping it simple*. Mom didn't *say much* about money, and I never heard my parents argue about it.

Mary and Todd had identified several factors that had steered their styles with money. The messages they'd internalized that drove their simplicity motives had come in various forms from all four parents. At first glance, it may appear that owning their business was quite different than their employed parents. But their business and their plan to sell it symbolized – and would function – as a pension plan to them. While this wasn't a conscious dynamic, the similarities of simplicity meant a "lump sum at the end." The only problem was, unlike their parents' traditional pensions, the sale of Mary and Todd's business was not guaranteed. However, that philosophy enabled an overly dominant pattern of "Keep it simple."

With the help of the mindful money tools, Mary and Todd identified their simplicity motive and its origin. Now they were eager to modify it and gain some diversification in a retirement plan.

Go to the growth motive chapter to see that pattern discussed in more depth.

9

Money Motive #5
Virtue

Virtue Summarized: The virtue pattern is m*otivated* by moral excellence, even superiority at times. This pattern will typically *avoid* materialism. Wealth may be *"bashed"* out of a concern that it creates negative consequences such as greed. The behavior this can *drive* when it's overly dominant, is modest income with reluctance to grow higher net worth. This is due to uneasiness over the perceived negative traits of wealth. Financial abundance may trigger a sense of guilt and cause actions that sabotage financial security.

Virtue Strengths: Compassion with a desire to make positive contributions during your life is a profound strength of this motive. This pattern is known for feeling repelled by greed or abuse of power, which drives you to maintain consistently virtuous motives. Your priorities and choices with both time and money usage are guided by this concern for high integrity. Your work choices may favor charitable entities that pay modest incomes or rely on volunteer efforts. Other strengths of this motive are discipline and generosity. With a naturally selfless spirit, it can feel difficult or selfish to attend to your needs rather than ignoring them.

> **Compassion with a desire to make positive contributions during your life is a profound strength of this motive.**

Virtue Rascal/Challenge Areas: *Basher* is the money rascal named for *bashing*, or rejecting, consumerism, materialism, and other perceived selfish behaviors. When Bashers consistently avoid financial self-care, they may find that, after a lifetime of modest living and generosity toward others, they're severely underfunded for their own basic needs. Their distaste for selfishness may have turned into *selfless*ness in the extreme. It's important these individuals honor themselves with permission to provide equally for their needs while they also pursue charitable or modest lifestyles. Self-neglect can bring more *austerity* than *prosperity*, and people with this pattern may eventually feel cheated by their self-imposed limitations.

Basher's Rhyme

*My name is **Basher** and I think wealth's bad,*
The chase for money really makes me mad.
The less I have the more I feel all right,
I keep life modest so I'll see the light.
To keep my money feels just plain greedy,
I'd rather give it to folks who are needy.

Emotional Drivers of Dominant Virtue Motive:

_ Charitable
_ Determined
_ Anti-materialistic
_ Righteous
_ Generous
_ Modest
_ Deprived
_ Affirmed
_ Resolute
_ Annoyed

As with many of the emotional drivers of the various money motives, the virtue motive "Top 10" list shows an inner feeling that's striving for one thing but occasionally receiving just the opposite. When virtuous motives dominate too frequently, it's possible to feel generous yet deprived at the same time. You can begin to resolve this by practicing balance that honors a desired outcome that's aligned with necessary self-care.

Virtue Motive Rebalance: To gain perspective, think about the origin of your preference for virtue. Have any of your life experiences left you with the message that you should always put others' needs ahead of your own? If so, explore what actions you can modify to keep an inner feeling of generosity, while starting to more adequately provide for your financial self-care. Remember to put yourself on your list of financial gifts! If you've discovered a tendency for being self-stingy, begin to be more generous with yourself. Another way to think of it is to include yourself in your budget!

In some respects, the virtue motive is the opposite of the prestige motive. Money is not used for power or material accumulation, so debt is rarely a problem. But a lack of savings or a passive acceptance of inadequate income may occur, which can cause an internal sense of insecurity, betrayal, or social unfairness.

You may need extra encouragement to take better care of your needs and, possibly, reduce charitable giving or other gifts if this practice leaves you with inadequate resources. This can become severely problematic when financial assistance to adult children, for example, is a recurring issue. In these cases, it may be advisable to discuss financial codependency with a therapeutic practitioner.

You deserve to be provided with the benefits of financial planning to build adequate funds. That is a positive thing and shouldn't be confused with greed or selfishness. Your natural talent for moderation in your financial life will help ease the way as you make a few adjustments. Challenge areas can arise if you've made too many sacrifices in your financial gifting or in laboring at occupations with modest incomes. You may have to revisit cash flow issues to support what is needed in your long-term planning.

It can help you **honor a balance** by using language that feels more virtuous to you, such as "financial health" instead of "wealth." Remember when you pursue your well-being, it contributes to other's well-being in the process.

Honoring Mindful Money Virtue Strategies: Empower greater financial generosity for your own present and future needs to honor yourself and your financial plan. This becomes the guiding light of awareness through your many life stages, preventing an overly self-sacrificing set of behaviors around money. When *virtuous* motives drive behavior too frequently, your choices become limited by the narrowed focus of avoiding greed or materialism. While this focus drives many positive decisions and good outcomes, it can become too self-sacrificing. Reflect on your deepest internal needs to make sure your generosity hasn't become an unhealthy identity of self-worth.

A Case Example of Virtue: Tom and Joy had been married for 15 years. Although they had no children, they enjoyed many children daily through their work. Tom was 42 and was the youth director at his church. Joy was 46 and worked in a daycare facility that specialized in preschool programs. She loved to say, "These little ones give great joy to Joy!" Joy was in a serious car accident while driving home from work and, tragically, passed away a few days later. She'd been the financial manager in their marriage; Tom hadn't paid much attention. Occasionally, Joy would review the finances with Tom, but he seemed to promptly forget the details.

Tom was devastated by his loss. He felt guilty that he wasn't somehow able to prevent Joy's death. Feeling lost in his own home, Tom was unable to open mail or prepare a meal. He was especially dumfounded when Joy's employer called to gently remind him that he was the beneficiary of her life insurance policy. Tom's immediate reply was, "I don't want money I want Joy!"

When a friend from their church visited Tom a few weeks after the funeral, he helped Tom go through some of the mail that had piled up. One of the statements was a life insurance benefit confirmation for policies on both Joy and Tom. He'd forgotten about those. Now Tom was going to receive even more money. The two policies together totaled $500,000. In stunned surprise, Tom remarked to his friend that he had no idea what to do. Tom shared his feelings of guilt and his impulse to simply make a charitable donation of the death benefit. He objected to the terminology, "death benefit," protesting that he did not want to benefit from Joy's death. His friend recommended a financial therapist to help Tom begin navigating the tough terrain of grief and money.

The financial therapist visited with Tom at her office. Kay expressed her deepest sympathy over his loss and began their session by explaining that the confusing mixture of feelings and thoughts Tom was experiencing were a natural response to Joy's death. Kay gently invited Tom to tell her a little about how his past few days had been.

Tom shared his feelings of guilt and shock. He said, "Everything has been so sudden. Joy is suddenly gone. I hate that there's no Joy in my life. And now I'm suddenly sitting here with money that makes me feel worse. What should I do?"

Kay responded with nurturing guidance, "The first thing to do is to set aside your urgency about doing something. It's best to hold off on large decisions if possible when you're grieving a significant loss." She advised that a financial expert could help determine what decisions, if any, needed immediate attention. Kay continued, "Give yourself some time to move through this emotional journey." Her advice gave Tom some relief, and he agreed to slow down. He understood that the life insurance money was in money market accounts, so it was safe and didn't need to be moved.

Kay asked Tom if he had any other unsettling feelings to share. He said, "Well, most of all, I feel like I'm going crazy." Kay assured him that he was not alone in that feeling, and asked if he'd like a simple summary he could read to help him feel less alone and less crazy, as he'd put it, in his grief. Tom was open to this, so Kay shared the **NEAR** acronym with him, going over the common experiences it represented:

Numb–**E**motional–**A**djusting–**R**ebuilding.

Tom nodded agreement and added, "I still feel numb and shocked at times. But as some of the numbness has worn off, the intensity of the emotions is almost unbearable. I almost want to find a way to bring back numb! I've had a few moments of feeling like I've begun to adjust, but then a few hours or days later, I'm lost in grief again. It's hard to believe these painful feelings will ever change. I hope so. I'm not sure what hope might be NEAR, but just seeing the possibility of it is comforting."

Tom and Kay continued meeting on a weekly basis for the next several months, reviewing Tom's perspective on where he was in the NEAR process. When he'd begun adjusting to the absence of Joy, he'd expressed an interest in moving forward to better understand his "prosperity personality," as Kay had described it. Tom said, "I'm glad that prosperity actually means well-being and not just wealth. I've noticed the guilt I felt a few months ago has diminished a bit, but I'm not sure what guides my direction."

Kay explained the concept of Mindful Money Motives and style patterns. Tom's most dominant pattern was the virtue motive, with a rating of 8. His peace motive was the next highest, with a score of 5 **(range 0–10).**

Kay asked Tom, "If you'd done this exercise a few months ago, do you imagine it might have been different?" Tom said, "Well, I think I was off the charts for virtue, but not for the right reasons. The grief tilted me towards total apathy, and that was driving my desire to just get rid of the money. In some way, I believed that would remove the feelings of guilt I had."

As Tom continued adjusting to his changed life, he began looking to the future again. He still mourned the loss of his wife, Joy. At times, he felt empty and extremely sad. But those periods began to occur less frequently, and the intensity of the emotion diminished over time. Together Kay and Tom explored his desire to **_honor a balance_** in his financial life, especially when he thought about what Joy would want for him. Virtue remained his dominant motive, but his control and growth motives had increased. He wanted to have a financial plan to help guide his choices about charitable giving, while taking prudent steps with managing his assets for long-term needs.

10

Money Motive #6
Security

Security Summarized: The security pattern is *motivated* by certainty and protection in financial matters. This will often cause one to *avoid* loss at all costs and perhaps *drive* spending or investing decisions that are quite narrow or limiting. Since absolute certainty or predictability is never fully possible, this motive causes worry – which is why its money rascal is named for being *"ashen"* and pale. Avoidance of loss at the expense of gain is the most common habit. The perpetual feeling of insecurity often dominates, even when things are going well. Security motives contribute positive characteristics also, such as pragmatism and discipline.

Security Strengths: Being motivated by security brings you many valuable traits, which can be stated as the three P's: Pragmatic, Pensive, and Proactive. This pragmatism drives frugality and discipline with money in many positive ways. It helps prevent impulsivity and the regret that can come from making snap decisions. This pattern is proactive, so procrastination is rarely a problem for you. Most likely, you established a protective nest egg early on and that serves as a reward for the "3P" strengths.

Security Rascal/Challenge Areas: *Asher* is the money rascal named for being *ashen* and pale from worrying about money. Asher's emotions range from mild uneasiness to severe panic. When the security motive dominates, your anxious thoughts may rule, even when things are stable and going well. To "Go it alone" is a poor choice when security is the motivational driver, because of the potential severe anxiety. The fear of loss has historically guided many of the security pattern's choices. It's important for the Asher styles to have a practitioner with an educational approach that helps you gain the security and confidence you need to make balanced decisions. Your impressive discipline and pragmatism is an asset in working with a practitioner. Professional advice, coupled with strong, customized financial information, will be of great assistance to you.

Asher's Rhyme

*My name is **Asher** 'cuz I'm ashen and pale,*
My money worries make me feel so frail.
Whether there's a lot or only just a little,
What I should do is such a freaky riddle!
So leave me be now, or I'll get upset,
It just seems money always makes me fret!

Emotional Drivers of Dominant Security Motive:

__ Insecure
__ Distraught
__ Vulnerable
__ Fearful
__ Non-trusting
__ Cautious
__ Discouraged
__ Powerless
__ Uncertain
__ Sad

> **Use financial analyses that compare your options so that you can honor what you need to help you feel more secure.**

As you can see by the "Top 10" emotions of the security motive, this can be an uncomfortable place to reside. Identify which of the emotions are most common for you. This helps you expand your emotional vocabulary and awareness of your internal money life. When you **honor a balance** by recognizing how to reconstruct thoughts that have fanned the flame of these emotions, your list begins moving to the opposite side of the emotional zone. For example, 'discouraged' moves toward 'encouraged,' 'insecure' becomes 'secure,' and 'distraught' turns into greater 'calm.'

Security Motive Rebalance: Be patient with yourself in your rebalancing effort. This motive is like the control motive in its desire for predictability. High security motives, however, often reveal an elevated pattern of fear, coupled with confusion about investments. Think about the kinds of worries you typically experience. Are they about income, spending, saving, or organization, or something else?

When you start to notice the pattern of your worries, determine to what extent they are fact-based. Often, worries can be eased by having an analyst quantify what's optimal, given the time horizons and level of income your savings need to fund over time. It can be very helpful to have several projected scenarios done, so you can see the sustainability of your financial resources. You can also request analysis about how likely different scenarios are to occur. Your prudence is a great strength and having good analysis can greatly increase your peace of mind.

Honoring Mindful Money Security Strategies: Use financial analyses that compare your options so that you can honor what you need to help you feel more secure. This is the best "way to weigh" the possibilities and be free of unnecessary and unhealthy worrying. When security motives always drive behavior, self-imposed limitations and narrow personal definitions of safety may be inaccurate, and cause excessive saving. This takes away from your enjoyment of things in the present.

Caution and discipline are strengths. However, it's important to assess whether your decisions reflect a lack of understanding about financial management in today's expanded universe of choices. Review what factors went into your previous decisions. Consider expanding your knowledge about diversification. Remember, savings and investments may cause purchasing power risk if they're overly conservative, which means they aren't keeping up with inflation. It's helpful to gain awareness from unbiased sources of how various investments function, and the potential financial effect on outcomes if you broaden your choices. This can ease old fears that may have arisen from outdated information or past experiences that are highly unlikely to recur.

A Case Example of Security: Ruby was profiled with her twin sister, Rosie, in the Peace motive chapter. Rosie was widowed and Ruby had moved in with her when they were 65. At age 70 the sisters sought therapeutic and financial guidance to help them resolve their financial differences and structure a better way to manage their money.

Ruby's Motivated Asset Pattern Assessment (MAPA) (**range 0–10**) revealed one predominant motive that drove her choices with money. She desired security above all else and as a single woman her whole life with limited financial education, she was driven to avoid loss above all. Ruby's strong preference was to act with caution to achieve as much certainty and safety as she could. This conflicted with her sister's top three motives: Peace, Spontaneity, and Control.

Ruby was retired and living contently on her pension and retirement savings when she moved in with her sister. In fact, Ruby's nest egg was more than enough to provide for her individual needs, given her modest cost of living. Her feelings of alarm and insecurity were triggered by Rosie's "undisciplined" money habits. When Rosie began asking Ruby for money, Ruby needed professional guidance to help her deal with their unresolved conflict and style differences.

Since Ruby had lived alone most of her life, sharing a home and expenses was a new experience for her. She was surprised and frightened by Rosie's inconsistent and risky financial choices. Ruby's inexperience with conflict, coupled with her high need for security, left her wondering if she needed to "divorce" her twin sister. In her work with the family therapist and her financial planner, Ruby realized she'd been feeling like she'd gone back in time and was reliving the unpleasant, conflicted life of her parents. She didn't want to fight about money, but she didn't want to lose her security either. Ruby's desire for security was greater than her desire to live with Rosie. She was willing to resume living alone, if that's what it took to regain her feeling of safety.

The identification of this boundary came from the use of ACE questioning (Ask–Confirm–Encourage). Given Ruby's history of hard work, discipline, and her retirement status, it was important for her to know her heartfelt boundaries and priorities. She was asked, "Do you want to keep your financial security and living arrangement with Rosie about equal in importance, or do you prefer one over the other?" Ruby felt the heaviness of this question, but couldn't quite choose. The therapist asked two additional questions to help bring clarity:

1. On a scale of 1–10, how important is it to you to protect your nest egg and financial security? (To this question, Ruby unhesitatingly scored it as a 10.)

2. On a scale of 1–10, how important is it to you to continue living with Rosie? (To this question, Ruby answered it with 7.)

The therapist confirmed Ruby's responses by summarizing for both sisters. "Ruby would like to continue living with her sister Rosie. However, she's not willing to sacrifice her financial security for which she's worked so hard. To continue living together, Rosie will need to modify those financial habits that threaten Ruby's sense of security. Thinking of yourselves as partners, you'll both need to have clear boundaries to help you find relationship harmony as well as healthy finances for each of you. Can you confirm if this is an accurate summary of your situation?" Both sisters confirmed this was an accurate appraisal.

Both practitioners then encouraged Ruby and Rosie to work together toward defining clear actions they would have to take to remedy the problems they'd encountered. With the practitioners' guidance, the sisters also defined how they would measure progress. They also determined when they'd reassess their level of satisfaction with their progress. Rosie agreed to continue with weekly meetings to help her continue adjusting her historic approach to money.

11

Money Motive #7
Control

Control Summarized: The control pattern is *motivated* by authority to regulate or restrain financial actions that threaten a sense of order. If control is a dominant style for you, you tend to crave organization, precision, structure, and predictability. Your behavior is programmed to *avoid* perceived chaos such as fluctuation in investments. This uneasiness may cause a preference for *"cash"* savings. Your top concern is for maximum future preparedness. These dynamics drive your actions to avoid debt and properly diversify investments.

Control Strengths: Control is an essential and important strength when it comes to financial management. This motive makes it likely that these individuals would be very organized and clear about income and cash flow. When managing money, these are extremely helpful strengths. Control-dominated individuals can pinpoint the location of their financial documents when necessary, and typically handle all details in a timely manner. No late payments happen with high levels of control! Saving money is also a top priority for you. In fact, you may enjoy saving money more than spending it, especially because of your distaste for debt. You'd certainly rather receive interest than pay it. You would typically like everything to be more predictable, so by keeping close track of things, you feel more in control. Your savings are calculated, but they may be overly conservative because of the discomfort you feel from the less predictable aspect of growth investments.

Control Rascal/Challenge Areas: *Casher* is the rascal personality that externalizes the control motive, named for its preference for *cash* control and savings. When this personality dominates decisions, it tends to favor frugal spending, calculated goal-funding, and conservative investments.

Cashers may experience an internal dialog that insists they keep track of every dollar (and possibly every penny) as the only way to avoid chaos and financial hardships in the future. The best professional assistance for this challenge area is to include "playful or enjoyable" items in your budget and demonstrate via conservative projections that your serious goals remain well funded.

Casher's Rhyme

*Hello, I'm **Casher** and I'm in control,*
No cash of mine gets lost in a black hole!
I track it, black it, I may even stack it,
If it's not safe I don't think I could hack it!
I save my money if I have my druthers,
And leave the risk-taking to all the others!

Emotional Drivers of Dominant Control Motive:

_ Calculating
_ Defensive
_ Controlling
_ Disheartened
_ Unyielding
_ Isolated
_ Frugal
_ Tight
_ Confined
_ Weary

If you identify with this pattern, use the "Top 10" emotions of the control motive to allow yourself to claim and tame your most frequently experienced emotions. Determine if the list triggers additional feelings for you, and identify them. This helps you begin to recognize the price you may have paid for an overly tight or restricted money life. Strike a balance by recognizing how to become more flexible while maintaining increased discipline. You'll find more pleasant emotions emerge, such as harmony and contentment. These can maintain the positive feeling of frugality without causing a total elimination of "fun" spending.

Control Motive Rebalance: If you have high control scores, you likely tend to desire predictability as much as possible, valuing discipline and order in your money life. Typically, you're uncomfortable with debt and have avoided it. Control motives are proud of discipline and structure. Discover if you've experienced "too much of a good thing" in this area. For example, if spouses have very different motives in this regard, it is valuable to discuss how you acquired your organizational style and how effective it's been. Work as partners to share strengths and utilize ideas from both styles that will be most effective for you as a unit.

> **If you have high control scores, you likely tend to desire predictability as much as possible, valuing discipline and order in your money life.**

Opposites attract, and control motives may often end up paired with spontaneous or simplicity motives. This can create conflict due to impulsive or inattentive decisions with partners on the other end of the money motives continuum. Review what has worked best for you and note which matters remained unresolved relative to the organization of your finances. If you have areas that neither of you are good at or desire to do, consider hiring a professional to do those tasks so remaining issues can be addressed and integrated into your future.

Honoring Mindful Money Control Strategies: When *control* motives dominate financial decisions, there are often many good results, including well-organized record-keeping and disciplined savings. This pattern, however, may cause a lack of enjoyment of the pleasurable things money can bring, due to a strictly narrowed focus on keeping money matters under perfect control.

If your focused efforts become extremely serious or commanding (especially in relationships), you may experience "too much of a good thing" if it smothers pleasurable aspects of life too frequently. To honor yourself, review the emotions in the Top 10 list, and consciously strive for some of their opposites. By releasing some degree of your control habits, you'll likely experience increased pleasant feelings such as joy and excitement.

A Case Example of Control: Let's return to Carrie, a new mother and the wife of Toby from the Spontaneity motive chapter. She and Toby were experiencing conflicts due to his impulsive spending, which was beginning to create debt. Carrie felt like she "carried a burden" in this dynamic of their relationship. Toby's impulsive spending clashed with her disciplined structure when it came to money.

Carrie's Motivated Asset Pattern Assessment (MAPA) scores showed one primary motive with three secondary ones **(range 0–10).**

> Control – 9
> Virtue – 6
> Peace – 6
> Growth – 6

Toby's MAPA revealed two primary motives:

> Spontaneity – 8
> Peace – 6

Carrie and Toby had made significant progress by using the **AHA** (**A**ction **H**onoring **A**wareness) therapeutic communication method. They recommitted to their goal of living within their means and gained new insights about their differing perceptions of what money had unconsciously meant to them, especially in matters of love. Toby formerly had looked for evidence of love through the giving and receiving of gifts. Carrie, on the other hand, felt love in a nearly opposite manner – to her, love was demonstrated by disciplined financial control.

Carrie gained additional insight from the "**COOL/FOOL** Rule." This helped ease her reluctance to communicate her needs to Toby. The COOL/FOOL Rule stands for **C**ulture **O**f **O**rigin **L**essons and **F**amily **O**f **O**rigin Lessons. "Lesson," in this context, refers to the conclusions individuals reached from the models they were observing. These conclusions frequently reside outside of conscious awareness. In Carrie's case, her primary new insight was relative to the positive harmony her parents displayed in their financial relationship.

Paradoxically, her parents' lack of disagreement about money had created an unconscious "rule" and expectation in Carrie's mind. She expected to be in automatic harmony with her husband in a similar manner as her parents had been with each other. When that wasn't happening, Carrie was completely baffled about how to confront the disharmony. She'd never observed her parents disagree about money. Consequently, she'd never seen them work through and resolve disagreements. When she and Toby had such different habits and emotional outlooks about money, Carrie felt paralyzed about how to find any resolution.

Carrie pondered the question, "In thinking about your family of origin lessons (FOOL Rules), what rules do you think you created and were trying to live by?" To this, Carrie found several mistaken beliefs at the root of her confusion. Many fit in the "should" department.

Carrie reconstructed the theme of her primary mistaken interpretations and rules:

From: Good marital partners should never disagree about money.

To: Good marital partners will disagree about money sometimes, *and* when that occurs, they resolve differences with respectful positive communication, understanding, and effortful compromise.

Carrie and Toby both found several subsets of their differing expectations about marriage and financial communication. They created written lists of their mistaken COOL/ FOOL rules and reconstructed them to serve as guides that reinforced the positive communication they wanted.

For communication tips that help resolve conflict, go to Chapter 13, "Conflict Resolution."

12

Money Motive #8
Growth

Growth Summary: The growth pattern is *motivated* by the desire to constantly increase financial results. Accumulating a *"stash"* of growth-oriented investments guides this motive to seek investment gains and higher net worth. This may cause you to *avoid* low returns or proper diversification and *drive* a pursuit of increasingly higher returns. Growth motives are quite positive, provided they don't demand constant growth to feel satisfied. That expectation can cause a pattern of loss if investments are excessively aggressive.

Growth Strengths: An admirable strength of this motive is your ability to create financial profits from many endeavors. You have a strong awareness of the importance of saving for future needs, and a strong preference for those savings to earn impressive returns. This serves growth-motivated individuals well, especially when calculated strategies and diversified choices are used.

When in balance, this pattern takes prudent risks to accomplish financial planning goals. Funding is also put in place to meet future needs. As with all the styles, the growth motive can drive you to go overboard if it's overly dominant. If the effort to gain higher and higher returns causes severe losses due to highly aggressive investments, seek advice for more diversified choices.

Growth Rascal/Challenge Areas: *Stasher* is the money rascal personality that externalizes the potential mischief in the growth motive. Stashers are named for their preference of *stashing* money in stocks or other growth-oriented investments in which they believe they can receive impressive returns. In extreme cases, this can lead to a preoccupation with daily trading in the pursuit of higher and higher gains. All too often this behavior leads to losses instead.

Stasher's Rhyme

*I am a **Stasher** and I say, "Let's grow!"*
Bank interest rates are dull, that much I know!
I don't spend much, I'd much rather invest,
And make great profits – that's what I think's best.
So, I keep my eye on the changing Dow,
And catch a ride that gives me a big Wow!

Emotional Drivers of Dominant Growth Motive:

_ Preoccupied
_ Dismayed
_ Focused
_ Stimulated
_ Driven
_ Knowledgeable
_ Restless
_ Competitive
_ Beaten
_ Aggressive

The growth motive's "Top 10" list reveals emotions that look almost like a stock market line graph. There are ups and downs that reflect the optimistic feelings when making certain moves to try and get large gains. Yet when the moves cause losses, your emotions reflect the opposite – down they go. Remember, the emotional drivers list reflects common feelings when the money motive pattern is highly dominant. When in balance, negative emotions diminish or even disappear, and positive feelings emerge. That's the benefit of honoring a balance.

Growth Motive Rebalance: If you desire to accumulate and grow your money well, it's especially important to allocate investments wisely without being overly aggressive. To reflect on creating greater balance, assess if your preference for growth is about the excitement of the pursuit to any degree. Money growth should be calculated based on asset classes and financial analysis, not for thrills. Determine your level of satisfaction from past investments, and on what that was based. Assess your true risk tolerance and be prepared for short-term volatility so you don't overreact or under-react to market news.

High growth motives do not necessarily indicate an aggressive investment portfolio is right for you. It reflects the *desire* for good returns, but your financial situation and risk tolerance may not be suitable for an aggressive portfolio. It's important to have a sound understanding of what it means in your investments when the market is down. If you've lost money by trading too often or too aggressively, it would be wise to adjust by integrating additional conservative strategies into your approach.

You may need to work on balance if you have any of these experiences: too much movement or trading to pursue higher growth; reluctance to spend; eagerness to spend earnings; unrealistic expectations about average rates of return; inconsistency about seeking and following professional investment advice.

Honoring Mindful Money Growth Strategies: When *growth* motives dominate financial decisions, a positive goal that began as a desire for a good return on investment may have evolved into unrealistic expectations and excessive risk-taking. While it is important for you to build growth into a carefully crafted investment plan, this goal needs to be kept in perspective and not exposed to excessive risk. The best investment allocation is unique for everyone. This allocation depends on multiple factors that include other current investments, employee benefits, age, health, time horizon of various goals, and lifestyle expenses, to name a few.

> **Review the importance of having your money available to you when you need it.**

If growth is a high motive for you, a thorough risk assessment can help you determine if there's excessive vulnerability in your investment mix. Review realistic expectations of various asset classes and help **honor a balance** between growth and stability of invested assets. Review the importance of having your money available to you when you need it.

A Case Example of Growth: Mary and Todd were profiled in the simplicity motive chapter earlier. They had been married for 20 years, happy and active empty nesters with a thriving consulting business. Both had doctorates in Organizational Development. They struggled to make ends meet in the early years of their business, and any extra money was invested back into the firm to improve its technology and marketing. They reasoned this was the best investment they could make. However, when they both turned 50, they decided to examine their retirement planning.

Mary and Todd's money motives were assessed and used to structure a conversation about their historic style and preference in financial matters. They knew they needed to "identify to modify" their desires, goals, or habits that were off track. Mary and Todd shared the same dominant motives, which reflected the busy, achievement-oriented life they'd lived together. Their schedules had always been demanding and full, which they found energizing. Their top two motivated asset patterns were the maximum rating possible **(range 0–10)**:

> Simplicity – 10
> Growth – 10

They had no retirement assets; their only savings was an interest-bearing money market account, which was established for emergencies or cash flow shortages in the business. They'd not had the market value of their business assessed, but they felt optimistic about selling it when they were ready to retire. As attentive as Mary and Todd had been about growing their business, they'd been inattentive about their retirement funding.

Mary and Todd had similar upbringings. Both sets of parents had uncomplicated lives and didn't openly discuss money. Their parents had worked in stable jobs and lived on pension incomes that met their needs. Mary knew she wanted to be an entrepreneur, having observed her mother's dissatisfaction with an unfulfilling job. Todd admired his father's entrepreneurial spirit, even though his father was an employee, not a business owner.

Mary and Todd consciously pursued growing their business as the way to provide for retirement needs down the road. They'd neglected to verify their assumptions, however. Their risk was extremely high, given they'd kept their investment strategy simple to the point of "putting all their eggs in one basket." Reinvesting all their money into their company was equivalent to owning one stock forever and assuming it would never fail and would always provide for their income needs.

This is a common "all-or-nothing" cognitive distortion thought pattern that exists with such assumptions and actions. It is oriented to high growth, but the risk is excessive when there are no other assets to use in the event selling the business fails. The TWEDY question they addressed first helped them assess their readiness to modify their previous habits. They knew they might feel some discomfort with making changes, so they pondered the question, *"To what extent do you* feel ready to redirect some of your company's revenue to a more diversified set of investments?"

Mary answered first, stating simply, "I think if we find a financial planner with an educational approach, we'll be able to ease into making modifications. I'm ready for that. I'd also like to take some steps to find out what our business might be worth on the market, and factor that into a plan. I don't think our optimism is enough to support us financially. It would be disastrous to discover we can't sell the company at all. I don't want that to be our only plan."

Todd admitted he felt skeptical, but like Mary, he wanted to see what it meant to be diversified. He said, "My main concern is that we stay growth-oriented. When I think about it, I realize that relying on the sale of our company exclusively for our retirement income is taking excessive risk. As much as I love our company, that degree of risk-taking is too much of a good thing. I'd like to dial our growth motive back from a 10 to a 7 or 8. With education and good advice, we'd not only modify our pattern, we'd rectify mistakes we've made."

Now that Todd and Mary non-defensively claimed their money motives and some of the money rascal mischief of their pattern, they could follow a plan of financial literacy education first. They'll follow that with a more diversified approach to their retirement savings plans.

13

Conflict Resolution

Opposites Attract *and* Clash

Before we married we were fine with money,
But now what I am seeing isn't funny.
The fun's not fun now that my date's my spouse.
We can't even save enough for a house!

I'm scared I might not have done the right thing,
What kind of problems might this marriage bring?
I thought we shared the same philosophy,
But what that means, we simply can't agree.

It has often been said that opposites attract. This is frequently the case with money styles. In short, the very thing that may have been part of the attraction in courtship can turn into the source of conflict, irritation, and clashing when money life is merged. Whether individual accounts are literally merged or not, a couple becomes a financial unit. What each member of the unit does will affect their unit's financial reality.

For example, a cautious penny-pincher may enjoy the fresh excitement in a new relationship with a flashy spender. Using money rascal language, their engage-ment headlines might read, *"Flasher spices up life for Casher!"* Casher is the rascal whose style prefers predictability and cash control. A casher style may subconsciously have the view that when it's someone else's money disappearing to extravagant out-ings or luxurious gifts, the courtship is exciting. It's a way for Casher to loosen up a bit, compared to the usual disci-plined restrictions with money. But when they marry, it's no longer someone else's money getting eaten up, and soon Casher is way beyond the old comfort zone. The excitement wanes quickly and becomes resentment.

> **For example, a cautious penny-pincher may enjoy the fresh excitement in a new relationship with a flashy spender.**

Certain themes occur with style clashes:

- One rascal cannot understand from where the other is coming (but doesn't openly inquire or listen, either).
- One or both partners rigidly believe their way is the only right way to be, and the other person should change or the marriage is over.
- They've never discussed goals, expectations, priorities, histories, or preferences with money management.
- One or both expect the other to "tend the tender," thus leaving it generally unattended.
- They discover they have conflicting philosophies and don't know how to resolve the difference.
- One feels superior or more qualified than the other, and wants all the control and power with money.

Even when two similar money styles get together, one might emerge as the champion spender, saver, worrier, etc. This is because of a natural comparative process that occurs between two individuals.

Another subconscious pairing that can occur is when an individual is attracted to a style with which they feel familiar, such as that of a parent's. Ironically, familiarity doesn't necessarily mean preference. A son may have resented his father's tight money management, for example, yet is attracted to a mate who manages money similarly.

Invisible belief systems are the reason it's so important to seek clear self-awareness about your money life. Otherwise, you may find you've been on auto-pilot with your finances without ever having identified your true priorities and values.

Gaining prosperity clarity is the key to money harmony in relationships.

Conflict Resolution Tools

Comprehensive conflict resolution and intervention is beyond the scope of this book. However, the CHAT process and conflict information in the next few pages can be a helpful resource for couples. They can be very useful especially if most of the ingredients listed for handling conflict well are present (see "Recipe for Resolving Conflict" in this chapter).

If, on the other hand, these attributes are already missing in the relationship, then the intervention and assistance of a good counselor is recommended. This can help resolve persistent, stubborn, or intensive arguments. A marriage counselor can also facilitate learning to communicate in new ways, so that everyone is heard and goals can then be discussed and agreed upon.

In addition, please refer to, "The Money Rascals Get Married" poem on the following pages for a rhyming look at how the money rascals may pair up when opposites attract. Try to locate themes you can relate to and identify the motives in each. Perhaps you'll find you're able to even chuckle at yourselves for a little therapeutic relief, and then begin trying the methods for conflict resolution.

The Money Rascals Get Married

When we were courting, my date brought such fun,
I was the practical bookkeeping one.
I'm still a *Casher*; I want money safe,
But at this rate I'll be a homeless waif!
The fun's not fun now that my date's my spouse,
We can't even save enough for a house.
It's easy to save money and keep track,
So why can't my partner stay in the black?
This stranger used to like my cash *control*,
But now I'm supposed to play some other role.

I am an expert when it comes to shopping,
But now it's me my spouse has thoughts of dropping!
I find great sales and gadgets for us both,
Yet now I'm asked to take a savings oath.
A faithful *Rasher* couldn't dream of such,
I need rash spending as my impulse crutch.
I can't imagine any other way,
Than *spontaneity* with all our pay.
And if my mate is not content with that,
Our marriage will be done in no time flat!

Before we married we were fine with money,
But now what I am seeing isn't funny.
A *Basher* knows selflessness is the key,
And life should be lived very modestly.
I value *virtue* to guide what I own;
Now my mate's doing things I don't condone!

I thought we shared the same philosophy,
But what that means, we simply can't agree.
I just want to make sure I'm a good soul,
And share that with a partner, that's my goal.

Yahoo! I'm *Flasher* and I've found a mate,
Good looking, well-trained, and makes me look great!
My spouse looks so good tucked inside my arm,
I get to have my way so what's the harm?
Give me *prestige* and let me spend for two.
I just don't get why that makes my mate blue.
What is the problem with a little debt?
I don't know why there's any need to fret.
As long as I'm the center of attention,
There's nothing else even needing mention!

Exciting, yes, I'm going to get married!
What better reason to feel rushed and harried?
It is my *Dasher* way to dash about,
And not leave time for any kind of doubt.
Sometimes my mate can dash along with me,
But then wears out and will just let me be.
I hope my spouse can organize the money,
I'm much too busy; I want *simplicity*.
I'm sure it all will work out fine and dandy,
As long as someone else is fiscal handy!

I'm scared I might not have done the right thing,
What kind of problems might this marriage bring?
It wasn't easy going it alone,

But now I'm in an unfamiliar zone.
Because I'm *Asher*, worry takes its toll,
And leaves me feeling quite out of control!
I wish my mate could take the fear away,
Then I'd have *security* in my day.
If only I had automatic money,
I might be able to enjoy my honey!

I love my spouse but when it comes to money,
My outlook's better; it is bright and sunny!
As a smart *Stasher*, I am in the know;
I'm sure I'll make our money really grow.
When I'm accused of getting carried away,
My answer is to promise big, future pay.
There's no good reason to slow down our stashing,
Not even if we take a major thrashing.
It's worth it for the *growth* that it could bring,
Even if it brings some marital sting!

I chose a marriage partner, good for me!
Then why do sometimes I just want to flee?
Being a *Clasher* is tough on a mate,
Like nibbling on some awful, rotten bait.
At first you think you're into something good,
But then, "should not" switches right into "should."
I need some *peace* and wish I knew our goals;
Perhaps then we could start to have controls.
If I am saving, then my spouse is spending,
Our inconsistency is never ending!

When things start to look SHADY

As the poem reveals, the money rascals start to cope in shady, or unhealthy ways when paired with an opposite style. The acronym **SHADY** (Sneak, Hide, Avoid, Deceive, Yell) refers to coping behaviors that sabotage healthy money communication in relationships. Conflict will most likely escalate unless new ways of dealing with financial differences are found.

The SHADY coping tendencies put some aspect of the relationship in the dark, blocking the light – or bright side – that could exist in a healthy relationship. Deception, aggression, or avoidance may bring temporary relief, but almost never result in a harmonious or productive outcome.

> **When things get SHADY with money,**
> **it's time to seek conflict resolution.**

At times, much of the problem is due to confusion or uncertainty about what financial steps are best for the couple. In these cases, a financial planner is a beneficial resource and can help you clarify the multitude of choices and needs.

The tools offered in this book are designed to help you understand yourself as an individual first. Then begin to make any adjustments you feel you need to enhance financial and emotional outcomes. When both members of a couple can do this, and begin to think about money in a new way, they can open the door to an improved manner of talking about it.

By examining your emotions and belief systems, you enhance your understanding of how you've interacted as a couple in your financial life. It helps you fend off defensive reactions or arguments when both members comprehend and honor the underlying force of each other's styles with money.

When two people begin to adjust their own dominant tendencies, making compromises becomes easier. The old SHADY ways are ruled out and CHATs (Communication Honoring Amended Tendencies) become the new, positive norm.

Next, review the communication tools on the next few pages and give them a try.

Recipe for Resolving Conflict

Ingredients needed to enhance communication and find solutions:

Communication Style
- Openness and authenticity.
- Listening for understanding, not for preparing what argument to make next.
- Ability to admit when one is mistaken.
- Absence of defensiveness and competition.

- Recognize and affirm each other when problems are resolved.

Mutual Objectives
- Desire for harmony and comfort in the relationship.
- Willingness to spend the time required to resolve the issue.
- Determination to deal with conflict, rather than neglect it.
- Both partners have an attitude of giving and receiving.
- Focus on the partnership winning, rather than one person or the other.
- Agreement that disagreements happen, but it does not mean that one is fully right and the other is fully wrong.
- Guiding objective is to admit what doesn't work (rather than who's right or wrong) and identify new ways to find fresh solutions.

Feelings
- Respect for self and partner.
- Enthusiasm for finding solutions.
- Appreciation of partner's uniqueness.
- Desire to keep the relationship free of resentment.
- Belief in your compatibility as a couple.
- Willingness to forgive mistakes.

Realistic Expectations
- Differences in opinions and style.
- Each partner makes mistakes from which both can learn.

Couples have a much greater chance of resolving conflict when they have learned how to combine the above ingredients when differences arise. If some of these are absent in the relationship, the **CHAT** exercises can help. Blending all the ingredients together creates a more harmonious partnership and an enhanced ability to adjust when needed.

Money CHAT Guidelines

Brief discussions about money in these exercises are called a CHAT. Therapists advise keeping initial talks as brief as 3-5 minutes while you learn the process, especially when you know it's a "hot topic" with conflicts from the past. You may need a therapist to guide you in this process when you're first learning it.

Begin and end each chat with something positive about each other. It can be something you appreciate about your partner, or an expression of gratitude for something about them. See examples below. Negotiations to modify behavior should only be done after CHAT themes have been confirmed and understood. The objective is to respectfully amend communication patterns that are ineffective for you as a couple. That's why CHAT stands for **C**ommunication **H**onoring **A**mended **T**endencies.

Pre-CHAT Starters

Choose and complete one of the following sentence stems to establish a respectful atmosphere before you begin your CHAT (as you gain experience in the process, you'll likely come up with some of your own):

- I look forward to experiencing this ...
- One of the things I enjoy most about you is...
- I've always been grateful for your...
- One way we make a great partnership is...
- I'm thankful for your special ability to...
- One of the ways you've helped me grow is...
- We work well together when we...
- I feel valued when you...
- I appreciate this about your money behavior...

CHAT Discussion Guidelines

There are three possible themes of a CHAT:

- Sharing difficult thoughts or feelings;
- Sharing neutral thoughts or feelings;
- Negotiating change.

Use the process below for each theme, working up to negotiating change for solutions to try.

Speaker: Share in advance the theme of the talk you wish to have, then ask if your partner is willing to listen for understanding (1st goal is understanding). Wait for a response. Accept a no as well as a yes.

Listener: Answer yes only if you will listen with an open mind and will resist interrupting and anticipating responses. If you answer no, you must initiate the CHAT later, usually best if done within 12-24 hours.

Speaker: Limit CHAT to an agreed upon time limit (usually 3-5 minutes), being as efficient in the message as possible. Use "I" language as in, "I feel [emotion] when [action]. Say, "I'm finished" when you've completed expressing your message.

Listener: Mirror or paraphrase back what you heard being expressed, then ask, "Have I understood what you intended?"

Speaker: Respond to mirroring with yes, no, or a restatement to clarify any part of your message that was received inaccurately.

Listener: Mirror message again until speaker affirms the CHAT was understood accurately.

Post-CHAT Summaries

After talking about each issue, always recognize positive aspects of what went well, then validate with encouragement.

- I think we made progress in discussing...
- When we can converse this way, I feel encouraged to...
- I am thankful for your sharing this with me...
- I appreciate your listening to...
- I think we should be proud for accomplishing...
- What I'm proud of about the effort we've made today is...
- One of the things I appreciate about your effort today is...
- Some of the important awareness I've gained about myself is...
- I'm glad you told me ____, because now I'm aware of it, and can be sensitive to...
- Here's an idea we could use to reward ourselves...
- The main insight I got today was...

Sharing Money Experiences

Couples can benefit by sharing their personal histories about money. This is helpful when both can discover the expectations that may have developed earlier in their lives, and identify new ones they prefer to follow as a couple.

The focus is on how you want your joint perspectives to take aim towards common goals, not to blame others or each other for previously developed habits or erroneous expectations about money.

> **Begin and end each chat with something positive about each other.**

Use the suggested sharing below to better understand each other's journey, and practice using the GEM steps to find new meanings that can help you both move forward honoring your new insights.

Money habits of the people who raised me:
- Spending behaviors...
- Saving behaviors...
- Conversations and atmosphere about money I noticed...
- Allowances or money flow with children...

My early recollections about money:
- My handling and feelings about it...
- Of other family members...
- Of friends...
- Of church or school teachers...

The rules or expectations I came to have:
- From people I admired...
- From past conflicted relationships (unhelpful or helpful habits I observed) ...

What I hoped money would create for me:
- Success
- Significance
- Social acceptance
- Family approval
- Control
- Happiness
- Independence
- Personal value
- Security
- Love
- Freedom
- Power
- Respect
- Serenity
- Other:

In what ways do these contain unrealistic expectations or distortions about money?

My money traits now:
- My primary values about it...
- My management style with it...
- Traits I want to keep...
- Traits that caused problems...

- Traits I'd like to amend...
- Ways you can help me modify old habits...

In previous relationships (if relevant):
- I was good at (or appreciated for) ...
- We seemed to be incompatible regarding...
- My main mistakes were...
- I think my previous partner's main mistakes were...
- Boundaries about my tolerances that I learned...
- Fears I developed that I want to resolve...
- There wasn't enough of this (or there was too much of) ...

New interpretations of the past:
- I'd like to modify my expectations about money to...
- I can see some of the models I observed were not helpful, and I want to change that to...
- I'm ready to create my own model with you, and it looks like this...

Goal Clarification and Alignment

Make separate lists of goals you have for yourself individually and for your partnership together. *This can include general career or income goals, housing, recreation, travel, retirement, children's education, community or church involvement, relationship goals or health goals (physical, mental, or spiritual).*

> **Make separate lists of goals you have for yourself individually and for your partnership together.**

1. For each goal, rate it on a 1-10 scale for degree of motivation, with 10 being the strongest. Those you rate as 8, 9, or 10 represent ones that feel like necessities to you and do not feel optional. To give them up would seem like a sacrifice too great. Goals rated 5-7 are those you would like to achieve, but are more optional. It would be disappointing if they were not met, but not devastating. Finally, the goals you rated 1-4 are the "nice to haves." These are more like wishes that you could give up rather easily, but if things go well, you would know what to grab next!

2. Add the age by which you'd like to achieve the goal (write as A55 for age 55).

3. Indicate an estimated cost by the goals that require money. If you don't know the cost, but believe it will be significant, write a "$?" next to the goal. Put a heart or any other symbol you like next to the goals that feel good but won't cost money.

4. Share your goals with your partner, and be sure to abide by the CHAT guidelines. First, decide on two joint goals from each of your lists that you agree are high priority partnership goals.

Now, choose two individual goals from each list upon which you both agree. Do any of the joint goals conflict with any of the individual goals? Will time frames need to be adjusted? For example, if you both want to take a vacation every year, but you also want to retire early, how will that be resolved? Is there uncertainty about cost or what is needed to accomplish a long-term goal? If so, use a financial planner to help you determine cost projections and methods to increase the likelihood of reaching the goal.

Merge the remainder of your lists, prioritizing as a couple and discussing any differences that arise. Adjust the motivation scores or time frames if you discover that you have too much to achieve in too little time.

You may find you like your partner's ideas better than your own. Adjust and be happy with this discovery. If there are items you can't agree on yet, decide not to decide, and research instead. Or there may be goals that can only be accomplished if your incomes can be raised. If that isn't feasible, put them on "temporary cancel." That means you aren't necessarily giving up, but the way to get it done is not yet a reality.

Congratulate each other on the goals that are aligned and discuss steps you will take to make sure they happen.

14

ABC's of Raising "Fiscally Fit" Kids

The **ABC's** of raising "fiscally fit" kids stands for:

- **A**llowance
- **B**alance
- **C**harity

This system is a simple way to incorporate some positive money models for children of all ages. Studies have shown that when children are brought up learning and practicing some basic financial principles, it helps them significantly in managing their adult finances well.

Allowance

Allowances are one of the best ways to give your children practice at handling money. It's like a version of their first paycheck. By giving them the experience of receiving and managing decisions around money, they are better prepared as they get older. The amount of money is not as important as the lessons that are built in. Typically, an allowance is given weekly (but as your children grow into their teenage years, you can try bi-weekly or even monthly). It is up to you whether you require chores as a condition of your children receiving their "paycheck."

Some studies have indicated that a "no strings attached" approach to allowance creates a more valuable experience. You can keep the allowance modest, while building in optional chores for which a child can earn additional amounts. I suggest having a "good citizen" method. This means children have certain chores they are required to do without pay as good citizens of the household. From there, you can identify other tasks that they can opt to do (or are required to do), for which they receive payment.

Regardless of the structure you use, an allowance helps children learn to prioritize spending, and with your coaching, how to delay gratification by resisting impulse buys. In the United States, it is estimated that 60% of supermarket purchases and 80% of all others are impulse buys. If you have an impulsive rascal who tends to spend the entire allowance in one shot, it's important to not give in to providing them an advance on their next allowance. That reinforces the wrong lesson.

Balance

Balancing savings and spending is an important aspect of children learning to keep some of their income. Build in some automatic savings from your child's allowance. It is best to show them their savings balances and any interest they're earning, by keeping a written record.

Regularly add an amount that will be saved on their behalf. Again, you are the one who determines these sums. Using a simple example, if your child receives $10 a week in allowance, you could put an additional dollar into a savings account or piggy bank (for older kids, you can point out that this is 10% of their allowance).

You can create rules for the savings accounts. It can be defined as an educational account that only gets used for that purpose, or it can be a special purchases account. Some people like to have a "save to spend" account. You can also create more than one type of savings account. One could be for education, for example, while an additional one could be for accumulating money they might spend for larger-ticket items.

For older children who may be employed, they can begin to accumulate extra amounts for future education funding, or even retirement. Make sure they learn the time value of money saved using a financial calculator. Compound interest is amazing! Especially when long-term views are included. The most important concept is to use children's financial transactions as teachable moments that instill healthy habits down the road.

An additional idea that fits in the Balance category is optional savings. If your child opts to save some extra allowance, you can add that to their savings account. It can be very motivating if you add a matching amount to this positive decision. Like employee savings plans such as a 401K plan, you can match a portion or all the dollars your children opt to save. If you can afford to match their savings a full 100%, it provides great incentive. With older children and larger amounts, you can begin to discuss and perhaps participate in investments with some of their money. It depends on your goals, time horizons, and other factors that can be discussed with a financial planner. The important thing is to communicate to children the impact of their savings behavior. Show them on a regular basis how their money is growing.

In the Balance category, also, it's important to teach older children about the costly side of interest. Credit cards, especially, are problematic when this lesson is absent. Interest charges can mount quickly when balances are not paid in full. There are many online calculators that can illustrate this principle. Use several examples of "what if" for your children, so they learn the cost of borrowing money.

Charity

Build in charitable causes to your children's view of human and financial asset management, and their experience is widened further. You may choose to give money to a charity. By identifying it together, it expands the values' discussion. Charity can also be done by donating time, which is a resource that brings important lessons as well. When you lead by example, money management helps children move from "mystery to mastery." It also decreases the stress that can occur as young adults if they've never had practice handling money.

Money discussions can begin as early as preschool ages. With age-appropriate explanations of income, expenses, and saving, children gain familiarity and comfort. Think about a preschooler's perception of money exchanges. For example, if you drive up to an ATM and after the push of a few buttons, a bunch of dollars magically emerge from the machine, what do they think? Just for fun, ask them! You can also ask if they think you can get all the money you want from that machine. Chances are, especially with younger children, their answer is, "Yes!" This is the start of a great conversation you can have with your school-aged kids.

When you use the ABC's as a guide for raising fiscally fit kids, not only do they learn valuable lessons about money, but so do you! It can be motivating at any age, while creating additional useful practices that build greater financial security.

15

Brain Science & Mindful Prosperity

The material in this chapter was originally created as a special report to provide clients with a summary of how mindfulness practices can be integrated into their financial planning. Here, it's included as supplemental material about basic neuroscience, while also serving as a summary of the money motives and money rascals.

Mindful, in its simplest definition, means **aware *and* attentive**. It sounds simple, but achievement of mindfulness can be easier said than done. Our brains are powerful and in their effort to keep us safe and alive, they sometimes work against us. How can that be? More importantly, can we do anything about it?

The good news is yes! Neuroscience of the 21st century says the brain is "plastic." This 'neuroplasticity' of the brain makes it much more capable of change than was previously believed.

While presenting a comprehensive curriculum of neuroscience is beyond the scope of this summary, it will reveal several aspects of important information about how our brains influence us.

> **This 'neuroplasticity' of the brain makes it much more capable of change than was previously believed.**

The objectives are to:

- heighten your understanding of your brain's abilities and habits, so you can manage it as a co-operative partner in any quest for change you've identified in your life;
- learn to apply techniques that help you maintain positive, non-distorted thoughts;
- increase emotional intelligence to skillfully manage and process emotions;
- identify how to use these concepts for greater internal and external prosperity;
- assess core money motives and make behavioral connections for improved outcomes.

Terry Fralich, Licensed Clinical Professional Counselor, Educator, and Co-Founder of the Mindfulness Center of Southern Maine, shares, "Through the practice of mindfulness, we have the chance to free ourselves from old thought patterns that no longer serve us well and to create new patterns that support our health and happiness. This practice of mindfulness gives us the best opportunity to act skillfully and creatively with the understandable and very human negative emotions that frequently arise in us."

Two of the brain's primary areas, useful in understanding behavior:

1. Cerebral Cortex
2. Limbic System

The **cerebral cortex** is at the top of the brain and is known for regulating emotions. Cortex functions are the most evolved, giving us the ability to process information by considering options, and choosing a response. It is, therefore, the most useful in making mindful decisions. However, it is slower than the limbic system.

The **limbic system** houses the *amygdala,* which primes the brain and body for action. Sometimes called the "alarm center of the brain," it is our brain's primitive center for alerting us to danger, so that we act quickly to survive dangerous threats. The amygdala operates with greater speed than the cortex, which is vital when it is busy saving us from true danger. However, it is also known for some inaccuracy when interpreting whether an event is life threatening or not. When the amygdala is triggered, the emotions that instantly kick in feel exactly like those that we experience when faced with genuine emergencies.

Many of our life events are stored as memories in our unconscious mind. When current life events are like previous ones, the brain retrieves those stored memories at lightning speed. This brain activity also happens outside of our conscious awareness. Next thing we know, we've reacted instantly, per our brain's alarm trigger. We don't realize that our reaction might be coming from previous experiences that have been inaccurately interpreted and mistakenly stored as dangerous threats!

Adults who have been harshly punished for certain behaviors as children may have multiple triggers that illustrate this occurrence. They may feel alarmed by stern looks, elevated voices, or even physical posture. This sensitivity causes a misinterpretation of "danger" due to unconscious stored memories.

You can imagine how distorted or irrational some behaviors may seem given they're a response to the acute emotions and physiological sensations of a life-threatening event. The best news is we don't have to be powerless to irrational behaviors. We can manage our brain in a cooperative partnership.

Mindfulness is that cooperative partnership. It can teach us how to "catch our brains" in the act of an alarm response that has resulted from emotional memories. By learning to recognize strong, emotional reactions as those that have been triggered by our alarm center (and therefore, likely containing inaccurate interpretations), we can train ourselves to prevent irrational behavioral responses.

What we learn to do is stop and let our slower cerebral cortex catch up with the alarm system before acting on the strong emotional signal.

Physiologically, what happens is that by retraining our brains this way with several repetitions, we transform previous brain circuits with new neural circuits. Think of your brain circuits as pathways that deepen with frequency. When you catch an old response and purposefully choose to execute a different one, you're doing two things:

- Stopping the old circuit pathway from deepening
- Establishing new circuits and deepening them

Stopping the old pathway from deepening makes it easier to eliminate old habits. Think of it as a "rut" you're less likely to fall into when you've smoothed it over. In contrast, you effectively establish a new and improved rut (new neural circuits) by engaging in new habits. Repeat the new habits frequently and they'll deepen, making them easier to do over time.

166 | SUSAN ZIMMERMAN

> **What we learn to do is stop and let our slower cerebral cortex catch up with the alarm system before acting on the strong emotional signal.**

Human and Financial Assets

Asset is defined as *advantage* or *resource*. Both words can be very liberating when you incorporate them in your thinking. Financial assets are what most people think of when they hear the word asset. They include the monetary value of properties you own and the money you have in various accounts (or perhaps stashed in the cookie jar or under the mattress!).

We believe it's mentally healthy to have heightened awareness of what we call your "human assets" as well. Human assets include your many non-financial resources or advantages, such as important relation-ships, your talents, values, interests, health, and energy to name a few.

Think about what you would list as your human assets. To strengthen your appreciation of them, write them down. And remember that your human assets should guide what you do with your financial assets. You'll find that listing your human assets in writing elevates your sense of well-being.

Prosperity

Prosperity means more than just financial success. In fact, it encompasses both psychological and economic well-being. Simply put, it means a thriving condition. It's helpful to remember this comprehensive meaning as a springboard for your own success both internally (your well-being) and externally (your wealth). When you apply mindfulness techniques to your prosperity, you can gain significant improvement in both your financial and your mental wealth.

We all have historic styles and preferences in our money lives. We've learned certain habits through experience, modeling, and varying degrees of formal education. Now that you've read about how our brains process the meaning of events, you can imagine that it applies to financial events also.

When you establish a prosperity mindset, it makes it more natural to mold your behavior to align your values and goals. Our research has determined that financial decisions are driven by inner core motives. Motive is defined as a desire or need that causes a person to act.

Balance creates positive emotional well-being regardless of what your dominant motives have been. It's the key that can propel your prosperity to new and lasting heights.

> **When you establish a prosperity mindset, it makes it more natural to mold your behavior to align your values and goals.**

Motivated Asset Pattern

Your combination of motives creates your own unique pattern that we call "Motivated Asset Pattern (MAP)." Think of your motivated asset pattern as the MAP that serves as your guidance system in financial decisions. If you intentionally set it for prosperity, your MAP is much more likely to get you there!

The benefit in knowing your motivational pattern is that it strengthens your total prosperity, so that you're in a thriving condition both inside and out.

Some money motives reside outside your conscious awareness. In this respect, your own **E**motions and **T**houghts (E.T.'s) may seem *alien* to you at first. Due to our brain's processing, at times we don't recognize what drives our own behavior, choices, and habitual responses.

Bringing our inner motives into conscious awareness is the first step in taking mindful and attentive actions to create greater wealth and satisfaction in our financial lives. It's an important alignment tool to help create balance in our financial and human assets.

We've identified eight money motives to help you recognize your own unique and dominant patterns. Use the information below to do a preliminary self-assessment of the money motives that have driven your financial decisions thus far in your life. We've named them. Now you get to claim and tame them!

Keep in mind that each motive has a positive influence in your prosperity, as well as some that may create challenge areas. None of the motives are superior or inferior to the others. They're simply about your preferences. It's possible and sometimes advisable to adjust your preferences. That's what creates more of the outcomes you desire.

Claiming Your Money Motives

✓ On the list below, using your first impression, check which two or three motives strike you as top desires in your money life overall. It doesn't mean the others are not important to you, but that the top ones are typically higher priority to you.

Prestige: Motivated by social esteem or distinction.

Spontaneity: Motivated by freedom from constraint.

Peace: Motivated by calm and freedom from conflict.

Simplicity: Motivated by uncomplicated clarity.

Virtue: *Motivated by* moral excellence.

Security: *Motivated by* certainty and freedom from worry.

Control: *Motivated by* power to regulate or restrain.

Growth: *Motivated by* ability to thrive.

Think about your primary desires when making **Spending** and **Investing** decisions.

Put an **"S"** next to the motive that most dominates your **S**pending decisions.

Put an **"I"** next to your dominant desire with **I**nvesting decisions.

Your "S&I" choices on the list may be two different motives, or you may check the same one for both spending and investing.

Money Rascals – When a motive or pattern is overly dominant, we've named it for the type of mischief it may make in our money lives. They're described briefly below and are noted in parentheses in the taming section that follows.

Flasher has a *flashy* image consciousness;
Rasher tends to be *rash* or impulsive;
Clasher has *clashing* desires that conflict with each other;
Dasher *dashes* through an overloaded schedule;

Basher *bashes* wealth or materialism, avoiding greed;
Asher is *ashen* and pale from persistent worrying;
Casher prefers *cash* and predictable control;
Stasher favors *stashing* in high growth activities.

Now that you're more aware of your money motive patterns, view the additional information about each motive below. It reveals common behaviors from which you move *away* or *toward*. Think about whether any of them have become overly dominant for you.

The three processes discussed below help you in **taming** your motives to find greater balance and better results.

Be positively MAD About
Taming Your Money Motives:

Motive • Avoid • Drive

Motive – your desire for a certain type of internal outcome or result;

Avoid – refraining from choices that you perceive as uncomfortable;

Drive – actions that move you to get what you want (or prevent what you don't want).

Prestige: Motivated by desire for social esteem or distinction, has tendency to *Avoid* mediocrity...which *Drives* achievement orientation & affluent, sometimes *flashy* lifestyles *(Flasher rascal)*

Spontaneity: Motivated by desire for freedom from constraint, has tendency to *Avoid* discipline...which *Drives* creative ideas & impulsive or *rash* decisions *(Rasher rascal)*

Peace: Motivated by desire for calm and freedom from conflict, has tendency to *Avoid* conflict...which *Drives* cooperative compliance and inconsistent, *clashing* choices *(Clasher rascal)*

Simplicity: Motivated by desire for uncomplicated clarity, has tendency to *Avoid* details...which *Drives* streamlined methods, procrastination, or *dashing* through tasks *(Dasher rascal)*

Virtue: Motivated by desire for moral excellence, has tendency to *Avoid* greed...which *Drives* charitable inclinations & modest lifestyles that *bash* materialism *(Basher rascal)*

Security: Motivated by desire for certainty and freedom from worry, has tendency to *Avoid* loss...which *Drives* cautious contemplation, limiting choices, *ashen* from worrying *(Asher rascal)*

Control: Motivated by desire for power to regulate or restrain, has tendency to *Avoid* chaos...which *Drives* consistent savings, precise record-keeping, and preference for *cash (Casher rascal)*

Growth: Motivated by desire for ability to thrive, has tendency to *Avoid* low return... which *Drives* profit orientation and growth investing *stashed* in stocks *(Stasher rascal)*

Motivated Asset Pattern Assessment (MAPA) Profile Questionnaire & Report Online

If you've not yet taken the Motivated Asset Pattern Assessment (MAPA) online to gain greater prosperity clarity, financial and emotional well-being, that would be a great next step. It provides you with proven success strategies designed for ease of use and effectiveness. It's compiled from your responses to the MAPA questionnaire and takes just a few minutes to complete.

Your MAPA report will convey the strengths of your dominant motives, as well as their challenge areas.

Visit www.MindfulAssetPlanning.com for login information.

For example, some strengths of the prestige motive/ flasher money rascal are described here:

- A positive aspect of the flasher style is an energetic enjoyment of life's pleasures and social enthusiasm that often brings delight to others.

Your MAPA report shows the most common emotions and thoughts within each pattern, with strategies for optimal management. This helps you increase your emotional intelligence and vocabulary to enhance your understanding of your personal history.

Report Example:

- **Mindful/Positive Strategies:** When *control* motives dominate financial decisions, there are often many good results such as well-organized record-keeping and disciplined savings. You may, however, find a lack of enjoyment from the good things money can bring due to an overly narrowed focus on keeping money matters in perfect control.

- Be aware if your focused effort becomes extremely serious or commanding (especially in relationships). Being disciplined can be "too much of a good thing" if it smothers too many playful aspects of life. Ask yourself if you experience excessive emotional habits in the above lists. Attend to it by building in plans that allow you to experience pleasant feelings such as joy and excitement more frequently.

Many people find it behaviorally useful to have a visual image of an external character like the rascals with which they can identify. It makes modifying their problematic traits easier to do. For that reason, the money rascal connected to each motive is identified and described in your MAPA report. **Example:**

- **The Peace Motive's Money Rascal:** *Clasher* is the rascal personality stemming from unclear, *clashing* desires or goals. Some thoughts may originate from inadequate information or the absence of good role models earlier in life. You may tend to go back-and-forth in financial decisions due to conflicting opinions that come from multiple sources.

- With clarified goals that show funding requirements, clashers find it effective to "talk back" to the mischievous thoughts and emotions that may try to sabotage new behaviors. Use the positive persistence of this style in finding the right mix of professional guidance and financial analysis.

Mindful Money Benefits

You benefit when you "inspire a rewire" of your own brain neurons by practicing new habits, even if they are initially unfamiliar or uncomfortable. When you identify your desired outcomes, and take the actions needed to achieve them, the formation of new habits moves from effortful to effortless.

Use the money motives to make the connection of your specific "Prosperity Personality" traits, being mindful of past avoidances or drivers that need adjustments to create more optimal results for you.

Focus on the benefits of honoring the balance that you receive when you reduce any of the extremes that may have resided in your emotions and thoughts (ET). When they are no longer *alien* to you, your awareness and efforts will help you increase your prosperity – both inside and out!

16

Take Heart in
Mindful Money Matters

Throughout this book, the working definition of "Mindful Money" has been to be aware and attentive in all your money matters. It's deeply rewarding to grow your self-understanding and attend to it in new ways. The internal and external benefits far exceed the effort it takes.

When you're making financial decisions, remember to "take heart." At the heart of mindful money matters often lies the courage to change. Courage is the guiding force of living life mindfully in all areas. It's an awakening to our valuable life experiences. You may need to encourage yourself to continue your mindful effort. One of the definitions of heart is courage.

Courage does not mean the absence of fear. Fear, like most emotions, ranges on a spectrum from mild to extreme. On the mild end is uneasiness, while at the extreme end is panic or terror. Isn't it liberating to realize we can't have the empowerment of courage without feeling some fear? They're like two different sides of the same coin – you can't have one without the other.

With most financial planning analysis and decision-making, there is some uneasiness. This can often be attributed to the natural discomfort that stems from engaging in new or unfamiliar action. Don't let that uneasiness mislead you. If you've compared sound financial analysis and weighed your human asset factors into your choices, you likely have a grounded, reliable strategy. When you take heart, you're finding the courage to overcome whatever degree of uneasiness you may experience as you implement changes. This applies to many of life's challenging issues, not just the financial ones.

Taming the mischievous rascal characteristics in your fiscal life helps with the maddening absence of absolutes in the financial choices you face. A little taming effort can create a more reliable internal mechanism to help in making your financial decisions. This way you can prevent repeated problems and feel satisfied at the same time.

Taming doesn't totally erase all our dominant style tendencies. Think of it as taking control of the wheel and removing your money rascals from the driver's seat. While letting them ride in the passenger seat, they're still along for the journey and their input can be considered. But they no longer have the power to throw you off course. We all have habits that are deeply ingrained that will tug at us to some extent. It's not realistic to think we can throw them out of our vehicle entirely, but we can regain control of the steering.

By making conscious changes in your thinking and behavioral habits, it puts you back in control of the direction to which you're moving. What taming does is expand the previous comfort zone to include some new strategies that wouldn't have been possible otherwise. Sometimes this involves new learning about money to which you'd never been exposed before. By overcoming inaccurate beliefs that have misguided your money habits, a gentle taming can begin without maiming the traits worth preserving.

When our fiscal lives are in balance we gain a new sense of freedom. In balance, we honor our highest priority goals and values, instead of simply giving in to our urges. The result is a feeling of greater security and financial confidence for the remainder of our lives.

> **In balance, we honor our highest priority goals and values, instead of simply giving in to our urges.**

Throughout the past 30 years, I've written multiple articles that often include rhymes to help reinforce therapeutic concepts. I dubbed them, *"a-rhyme-a-therapy."* It's like aroma-therapy, except it's 'a rhyme' that contains the therapeutic component (rather than aroma). Rhymes, like acronyms, have a component that can help your brain retain concepts that matter to you. Here's one on the topic of fear and courage:

Faithful Courage

The path to courage is blazed by fear;
We can't have one unless the other's near.
Persistently, then, toward each we'll steer,
Embracing both and holding them dear.

As you pursue deepening your awareness of emotions, thoughts, financial well-being, and sound financial planning, take heart as you discover new insights and act to honor them. When you respect your genuinely healthy motives, you find compassionate prosperity from the inside out. Here's a bonus acronym for that concept:

"Be **NUTTY!**" – **N**ever **U**nderestimate **T**he **T**rue **Y**ou.

It's the 'true you' that propels you to take strong steps that honor your life's purpose. Your success, as you define it, is heightened. Your happiness and contentment deepens when you trust your ability to make a positive difference in your life and the lives of others. People need the true you to shine.

> **When you respect your genuinely healthy motives, you find compassionate prosperity from the inside out.**

There's always more to learn about others as well as ourselves. Take heart in the adventure! Bravely plunge in. Keep practicing and improving. It's impossible to be perfect, so strive for progress.

When mindful money practices help guide the way, you naturally honor a healthier balance with your important life and money matters!

References

Altman, Donald. *The Joy Compass.* Oakland: New Harbinger Publications, Inc., 2012

Bachrach, Bill. *Values-Based Financial Planning: The Art of Creating an Inspiring Financial Strategy.* San Diego: Aim High Publishing, 2000.

Benziger, Katherine. *Thriving in Mind: The Art and Science of Using Your Whole Brain.* Carbondale: KBA, LLC Publishing, 2003.

Burns, David, MD. *Feeling Good: The New Mood Therapy.* Penguin Books, 1980.

Curran, Linda A. *Trauma Competency: A Clinician's Guide.* Eau Claire: PESI, LLC, 2010.

Doidge, Norman *The Brain that Changes Itself: Stories of Personal Triumph from the Frontiers of Brain Science.* New York: Penguin, 2007.

Fralich, Terry. *Cultivating Lasting Happiness: A Seven-Step Guide to Mindfulness.* Eau Claire: Premier Publishing and Media, 2007.

Hanson, Rick. *Just One Thing: Developing a Buddha Brain One Simple Practice at a Time.* Oakland: New Harbinger Publications, Inc., 2011.

Hanson, Rick and Richard Mendius, MD. *Buddha's Brain: The Practical Neuroscience of Happiness, Love & Wisdom.* Oakland: New Harbinger Publications, Inc., 2009.

Hayden, Ruth L. *For Richer, Not Poorer: The Money Book for Couples.* Deerfield Beach, FL: Health Communications, Inc., 1999

Herrmann, Ned. *The Whole Brain Business Book: Unlocking the Power of Whole Brain Thinking in Organizations and Individuals.* New York: McGraw-Hill, 1996.

Jetson, Dave. *Finding Emotional Freedom: Access the Truth Your Brain Already Knows.* Rapid City: CreateSpace, 2013.

Kahler, Rick and Kathleen Fox. *Conscious Finance: Uncover Your Hidden Money Beliefs and Transform the Role of Money in Your Life.* Rapid City: FoxCraft, Inc., 2005.

Kahneman, Daniel. *Thinking, Fast and Slow.* New York: Farrar, Straus and Giroux, 2011.

Kegan, Robert and Lisa Laskow Lahey. *Immunity to Change: How to Overcome it and Unlock the Potential in Yourself and Your Organization.* Boston: Harvard Business Press, 2009.

Klontz, Ted, and Rick Kahler and Brad Klontz. *The Financial Wisdom of Ebenezer Scrooge: 5 Principles to Transform Your Relationship with Money.* Deerfield Beach: Health Communications, 2006.

Leitschuh, Cheryl. *Leadership Energy: Unlocking the Secrets to Your Success.* Bloomington: Balboa Press, 2013.

McEwen, Bruce and Elizabeth Norton Lasley. *The End of Stress as we Know It.* Washington, D.C.: Joseph Henry Press, 2002.

Price, Verna Cornelia. *The Power of People: Four Kinds of People Who Can Change Your Life.* Minneapolis: JCAMA Publishers, 2002.

Richards, Carl. *The Behavior Gap: Simple Ways to Stop Doing Dumb Things with Money.* New York: Penguin Group, 2012. *Siegel, Daniel. Mindsight: The New Science of Personal Transformation.* New York: Bantam Books, 2010.

Schwartz, Jeffrey MD and Gladding, Rebecca MD. *You are Not Your Brain: The 4-Step Solution for Changing Bad Habits, Ending Unhealthy Thinking, and Taking Control of Your Life.* New York: Penguin Group, 2012

Zimmerman, Susan. *Rays of Hope in Times of Loss: Courage and Comfort for Grieving Hearts.* Andover: Expert Publishing, Inc., 2005.

Zimmerman, Susan. *The Money Rascals: Changing Troublesome Habits from the Inside Out.* St. Paul, 1998.

Zimmerman, Susan. *The Power in Your Money Personality: 8 Ways to Balance Your Urge to Splurge with Your Craving for Saving.* Minneapolis: BP Press, 2002.

Zimmerman, Susan. *Mindful Money for Wealth and Well-Being: Help Clients Strike a Balance in Financial Planning.* Mindful Asset Publishing, 2014.

Zimmerman, Susan. "Mindful Prosperity: A GEM Guide to Mental Wealth." *Mindful Asset Planning.* (2012). E-Book free download at www.mindfulplanning.com